display creative literacy

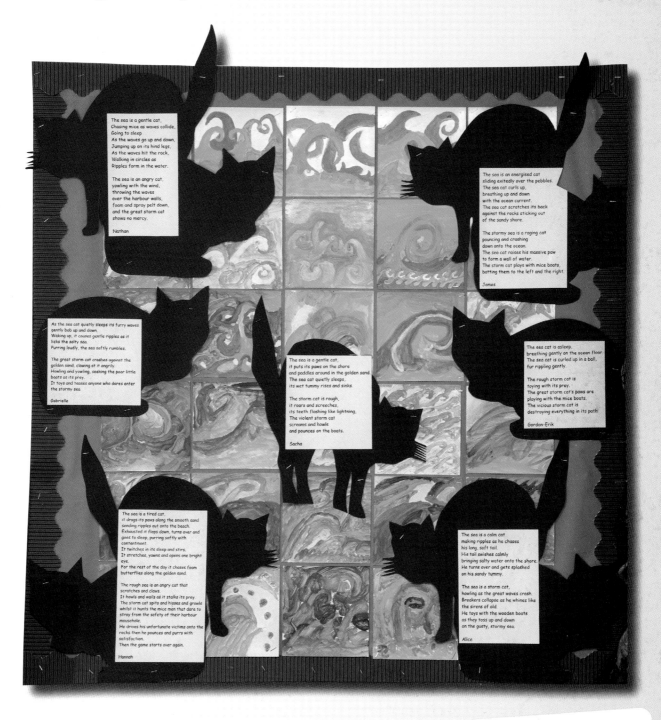

The sea is a gentle cat,
Chasing mice as waves collide,
Going to sleep
As the waves go up and down,
Jumping up on its hind legs,
As the waves hit the rock,
Walking in circles as
Ripples form in the water.

The sea is an angry cat,
yowling with the wind,
throwing the waves
over the harbour walls,
foam and spray pelt down,
and the great storm cat
shows no mercy.

Nathan

The sea is an energised cat
sliding exitedly over the pebbles.
The sea cat curls up,
breathing up and down
with the ocean current.
The sea cat scratches its back
against the rocks sticking out
of the sandy shore.

The stormy sea is a raging cat
pouncing and crashing
down onto the ocean.
The sea cat raises his massive paw
to form a wall of water.
The storm cat plays with mice boats,
batting them to the left and the right.

James

As the sea cat quietly sleeps its furry waves
gently bob up and down.
Waking up, it causes gentle ripples as it
licks the salty sea.
Purring loudly, the sea softly rumbles.

The great storm cat crashes against the
golden sand, clawing at it angrily.
Howling and yowling, seeking the poor little
boats as its prey.
It toys and teases anyone who dares enter
the stormy sea.

Gabrielle

The sea is a gentle cat,
it puts its paws on the shore
and paddles around in the golden sand.
The sea cat quietly sleeps,
its wet tummy rises and sinks.

The storm cat is rough,
it roars and screeches,
its teeth flashing like lightning,
The violent storm cat
screams and howls
and pounces on the boats.

Sacha

The sea cat is asleep,
breathing gently on the ocean floor.
The sea cat is curled up in a ball,
fur rippling gently.

The rough storm cat is
toying with its prey.
The great storm cat's paws are
playing with the mice boats.
The vicious storm cat is
destroying everything in its path.

Gordon-Erik

The sea is a tired cat,
it drags its paws along the smooth sand
sending ripples out onto the beach.
Exhausted it flops down, turns over and
goes to sleep, purring softly with
contentment.
It twitches in its sleep and stirs.
It stretches, yawns and opens one bright
eye,
For the rest of the day it chases foam
butterflies along the golden sand.

The rough sea is an angry cat that
scratches and claws.
It howls and wails as it stalks its prey.
The storm cat spits and hisses and growls
whilst it hunts the mice men that dare to
stray from the safety of their harbour
mousehole.
He drives his unfortunate victims onto the
rocks then he pounces and purrs with
satisfaction.
Then the game starts over again.

Hannah

The sea is a calm cat
making ripples as he chases
his long, soft tail.
His tail swishes calmly
bringing salty water onto the shore.
He turns over and gets splashed
on his sandy tummy.

The sea is a storm cat,
howling as the great waves crash.
Breakers collapse as he whines like
the sirens of old.
He toys with the wooden boats
as they toss up and down
on the gusty, stormy sea.

Alice

Céline George
Sue Dean

Acknowledgments

The authors and publishers would like to thank the children of Bishops Down Primary School, Claremont Primary School, Cross-in-Hand Primary School, Rose Hill School, Sherwood Park Community Primary School, Stonegate Primary School, St. Thomas' Primary School and Willow Park Primary School (Auckland, New Zealand) for their literacy work and artwork. They would also like to give special thanks to Sophie George, Christopher Dean, Jeannette Magee, Florence Granatt, Cherane Marshall and Julie Retberg for their expert help. They would also like to thank Amy Powderham, Rosie Stoward, Beth Dewhurst and Sammie Hibbard-Daniels of Tunbridge Wells Girls Grammar School for their expert help and enthusiasm.

The authors would like to thank these teachers for their expertise and practical help: Amy Follows, Becky Hunt, Caroline Powell, Helen Runalls, Alison Wilmshurst, James Green, Elaine Brooks, Amanda Rock, Jenny Hoellen, Joe Gerrard, Margot Davison, Michele Baldwin, Cari Reid, Jane Wilce, Sally Nixey, Rachel Crane, Liz Soar, Jonathan Clarke, Simon Bird, Sarah Chater, Jo Adams, Diana Jenkinson, Irene Campbell, Lucy Smith, Trudie Maxim, Lizzy Connors, Gretchen Baker, Liz Manson, Jane Clarke, Rosemary Appleyard, Mary Westhead, Wanda Wilson and Cliff Dean. They would like to give special thanks to Emma Savage and Keith Marden for their enthusiastic support and encouragement. Finally, they would like to thank Emma Bonwick, Matthew Sayer, Jo Salter, Kate Westcott and Kate Gudgeon for their creative inspiration and expert help.

Morocco – The Bachelor and the Bean (page 32)

Commissioning Editor: Zoë Nichols   Editor: Melody Ismail

Page Design: Philippa Jarvis   Photography: Steve Forest and Kelvin Freeman

Cover Design: Steve West

First published in 2007 by Belair Publications.

372.
6
GEO

Contents

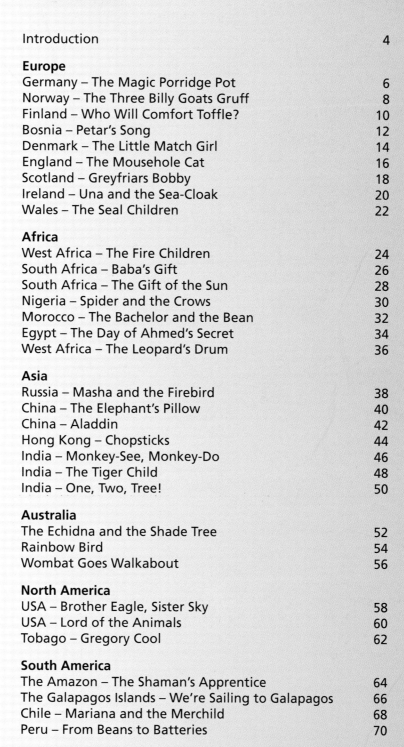

Introduction

Display Creative Literacy uses illustrated stories from around the world as starting points for creative work, with a special focus on literacy, art and design. The chapters are split into continents, containing themes linked to different countries. The themes explore a variety of literacy objectives such as story writing, poetry, speaking and listening, and drama. Often the learning is linked to a final piece, combining literacy, art and display. Many of the themes could inspire further cross-curricular work. We have linked all of the stories closely with curriculum requirements. Most of the activities are easily adapted for use with different age groups.

Using the Stories

The stories have been chosen for their illustrations as well as for their interesting content. There are stories suitable across the age groups 5–11. Often picture books are perceived as suitable only for younger readers, but in fact we have found that they can be used very successfully with older children as the themes explored can be extended and used on different levels. For example, *Lord of the Animals* is a simple creation story but the illustrations are very sophisticated, promoting discussion at a more advanced level.

We would suggest that, before reading each story, a world map or atlas is used to find the country where the story is set. This puts the story in context and can provide links with other areas of the curriculum, such as Geography. In addition, inviting visitors into the class, who are familiar with the countries where the stories are set, contributes an extra dimension and brings the setting to life.

Some stories were chosen because the illustrations are as powerful and emotive as the texts. We found that the children were highly motivated by the images and as a result their work in both art and literacy was enriched. In the story *Petar's Song*, the evocative illustrations are linked closely with the text and together they present vivid images of a war-torn country. For older children in particular, this enabled them to empathise with the characters in the story.

In many of the stories, the illustrations reflect a powerful image and often tell the story from a different perspective. For example, in *Una and the Sea-Cloak* the children wrote and performed their own play based on the story. The quirky illustrations inspired the striking set and costume designs and made the whole project a very innovative and exciting one.

The Themes

Each theme explores a different story. After general information about the story there are three activities, each exploring a different literacy objective culminating in a link to art or display. The activities could be spread over a number of lessons.

Many of the activities in this book lend themselves to discussion work in which speaking and listening are every bit as important as reading and writing. We found that when children were presented with opportunities to express their views about an inspiring text, the work was often outstanding.

We also found that by focusing on picture books that reflect a variety of cultures, the children's awareness of the richness that cultural diversity brings has been enhanced. The work has been engaging for children and teachers alike and the results have been spectacular!

We hope you enjoy using this book.

Céline George and *Sue Dean*

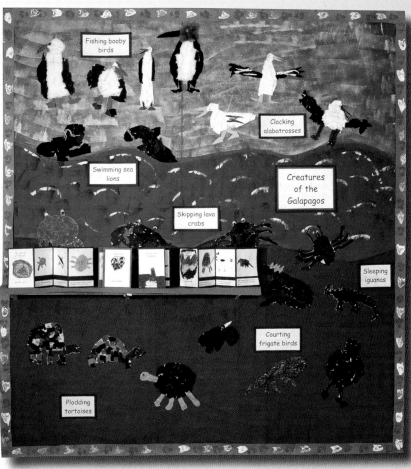

Germany – The Magic Porridge Pot

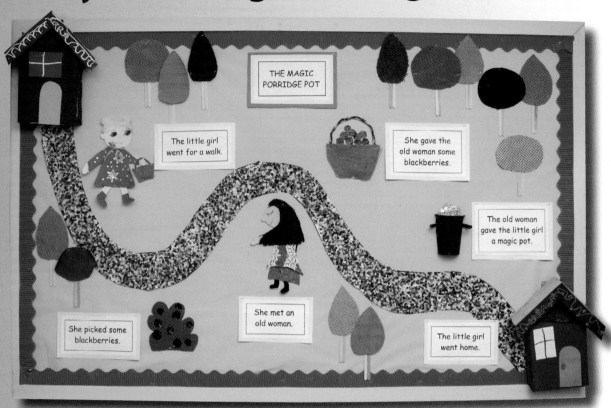

Read *The Magic Porridge Pot* from *The Story Tree: Tales to Read Aloud* retold by Hugh Lupton, illustrated by Sophie Fatus (published by Barefoot Books). This delightful story is full of surprise, fun and unexpected happenings. The story begins with a little girl who is hungry and decides to go out to find something to eat. She sets off with her basket and comes across some bramble bushes full of blackberries. On her journey, she meets an old woman who is dressed in rags and she shares the blackberries she has gathered. As a result of her kindness, the old woman gives the little girl a special gift of a magical, iron pot along with some very specific instructions on how to use it. The illustrations enhance the text: the wooden buildings, with elaborate roof carvings, reflect a very traditional German-style home. The characters in the story are illustrated in traditional dress. When the little girl's mother is unable to remember the words to stop the pot cooking, everywhere fills up with porridge!

The Journey

Approach

1. Discuss the purpose of the little girl's journey and the events that happened along the way. Mention how the illustrations contribute to the different stages of the journey by depicting a patterned path that snakes through the countryside.

2. Create storyboards showing the little girl's journey: starting from her house, meeting the old woman and returning home.

3. Ask the children to include captions to match the pictures on their storyboards.

4. Make a wall display of the little girl's journey using the storyboards as a planner. Use a variety of materials and include the winding path.

Resources
- A4 card
- A4 cartridge paper divided into six sections
- Colouring pencils
- Different coloured paper and tissue paper
- Variety of collage materials

Wooden Houses

1. Discuss the architecture of the houses. Mention the decorative features of the roofs and the wooden shutters. The furniture inside is simple, but colourful. Point out the wood burning stove, wooden table and chairs, vase of flowers and the brightly patterned bed cover.

2. Ask the children to make 3-D model houses by sticking corrugated card to cardboard boxes. Add the decorative features on the roof using strips of black or brown card and embellish with silver or gold pens.

3. Write two lists comparing the similarities and differences between the houses in the story and the children's houses.

4. Display the writing with the model houses.

Resources

- Corrugated card
- Silver and gold pens
- Cardboard boxes
- Strips of dark, thin card

Magic Pots

Resources

- Different shaped boxes
- Fluorescent paint
- Thin card
- Gummed paper shapes
- Feathers
- Pipe cleaners

1. Discuss the different types of containers and pots that children are familiar with.

2. Ask the children to create an exciting design for a magic pot and to make it using a variety of materials. They could use fluorescent paint, coloured paper shapes and feathers for decoration. Handles could be made using two pipe cleaners twisted together.

3. Discuss the consequences of using the magic pot in the story. Then ask the children to write instructions for how to use their own pots, including what will happen if the instructions are not followed!

4. Display the magic pots with the children's instructions.

Norway – The Three Billy Goats Gruff

Read *The Three Billy Goats Gruff* from *The Story Tree: Tales To Read Aloud* retold by Hugh Lupton, illustrated by Sophie Fatus (published by Barefoot Books). This traditional tale tells the story of how the three Billy Goats Gruff outwit the gullible Troll in order to reach the thick green grass on the other side of the deep river. The old Troll who lives under the bridge is hungry and on hearing the first Billy Goat Gruff 'trip trap' across the bridge, leaps out wanting to eat him. The wily goat tricks the Troll and is able to cross the bridge as does the second Billy Goat Gruff. When the biggest goat arrives, the confrontation is resolved by force, and finally all three Billy Goats Gruff are able to enjoy the grass on the hillside. The humorous illustrations depict the Troll licking his lips in anticipation, as the goats travel across the bridge.

The Troll

Approach

1. Discuss what a troll is (a mythical creature from Scandinavia) and the role he plays in the story. Discuss his appearance and features.

2. Ask the children to write a description of a troll, to include details about his personality, what he looks like, where he lives and what he likes to eat.

3. Using their descriptions, children could make a picture of a troll, using a variety of fabrics and techniques.

4. Children could then make small models of troll heads using clay. Paint and embellish using a variety of craft materials.

5. Display the troll heads in front of a river setting. Make a bridge using large paper clips and use shiny coins to depict the sun. Place the descriptions of the trolls on the display.

Resources
- Clay
- Junk and craft materials
- Glue
- Paint

Three Billy Goats

Approach

1. Discuss the difference in size between the three goats and how the first two goats tricked the Troll into letting them cross the bridge, and how the biggest goat resolved the problem.

2. Ask the children to make the three Billy Goats Gruff in different sizes (small, medium and large), using string, sugar paper and collage materials.

3. Re-tell the story using models of the goats and the Troll. Take photographs to illustrate the stages of the story.

4. Display the photographs with the story.

Resources
- Sugar paper
- Strips of sugar paper in assorted colours
- String
- Crayons and felt pens

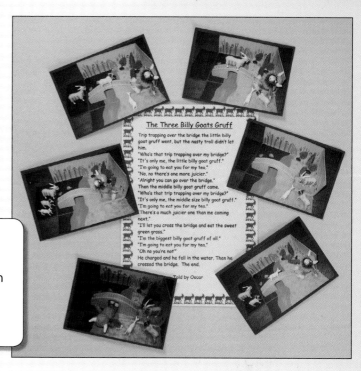

The Landscape

Approach

Resources
- Backing paper
- Sugar paper
- Tissue and crepe paper
- Gummed paper
- Paint
- Fabric

1. Discuss the Norwegian landscape as depicted in the story (the houses and barns traditionally made from wood and painted red, and the pine trees typical of a colder climate). Compare this with your own climate.

2. Make a collage showing the contrasting landscapes of the rocky, barren side from which the goats were trying to cross the bridge, into the lush, green grass on the other side. Use a variety of materials for the display.

3. For the goats, use strips of different-coloured paper rolled on a pencil for a 3-D effect. Make the horns by folding paper into a long cone shape and draw on the ridges of the horns using a felt pen.

Finland – Who Will Comfort Toffle?

Brave **Toffle** crept through the deep, dark wood, feeling as brave as he possibly could.

Around every tree eyes would peer, fearing danger coming near.

Toffle heard the sound of many things, like bats flapping their big, black wings.

He heard hedgehogs snuffling in the leaves, which made poor **Toffle** wobble his knees.

The hedgehogs, finding their food had gone, kept rustling the leaves and scuttling on.

He heard the scratching of little mice; their eyes peeping out as white as ice.

An old pine tree standing alone gave a cracking kind of groan.

Owls do make a horrible sound, but they held **Toffle** quite spellbound.

A bat swooped past scared **Toffle**'s head, its claws were stained a ghastly red.

So poor old **Toffle** trudged through the wood, feeling as brave as he possibly could.

Read *Who Will Comfort Toffle?: A Tale of Moomin Valley* by Tove Jansson (published by Sort of Books). This book is set in an imaginary landscape and the images in it resonate with Scandinavia and, in particular, Finland. The main character, Toffle, is lonely and feels isolated from others because of his shyness. The illustrations are quirky, imaginative and reflect a very different setting full of dream-like characters such as the Moomins. Some of the illustrations are predominantly dark with a hint of colour and others are highly decorative and colourful, often with a white background. The decorative images are reminiscent of the designs used for the Finnish company, Marimekko, which are bold, colourful and eye-catching. In most of the illustrations the author has written her first name (as an artist does on a painting) and interestingly Tove Jansson was an artist before she became a writer. Towards the end of this delightful story, Toffle finds a bottle with a message in it from someone who is even more scared of people than he is. Through his bravery and kindness, Toffle overcomes his shyness and discovers the fun that true friendship brings.

The Forest

Approach

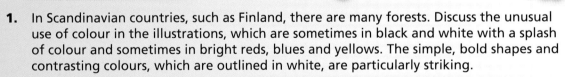

1. In Scandinavian countries, such as Finland, there are many forests. Discuss the unusual use of colour in the illustrations, which are sometimes in black and white with a splash of colour and sometimes in bright reds, blues and yellows. The simple, bold shapes and contrasting colours, which are outlined in white, are particularly striking.

2. The children could make a variety of 3-D images taken from the forest scene. Using black card outlined in white for the trees, the children could then add bats, hedgehogs, treetop houses and an anxious looking Toffle.

3. In the poem, the names Toffle and Miffle are always written in bold and the structure of the poem is in rhyming couplets with a definite chorus. Write a collaborative, narrative poem using the same style and setting. Focus on another episode in the story.

4. Place the enlarged poem as the focus point of the display with images from the forest scene around it. In this example the display was created within a cardboard box.

Resources
- A variety of coloured card, including black and white
- Red and white poster paint
- Silver or white pens
- White cartridge paper

The Carousel

Approach

1. Discuss the illustration that shows Toffle looking at the Whompses on carousels, dancing and lighting fireworks. Discuss the use of contrasting colours to depict the busy scene.

2. Produce a collaborative painting of a fairground scene on black card. Include a variety of activities such as carousels, children eating candyfloss, riding in giant cups and saucers or holding colourful balloons. Restrict the paint palette to white, red, yellow and blue. Aim to create a magical, night time scene using acrylic paints to add bright colours.

3. Ask the children to write a descriptive piece using powerful language to bring the scene to life. Include a description of the different rides and how the children might feel about going on them.

4. Display the fairground painting with one of the pieces of descriptive writing.

Resources
- Black card
- White, red, blue and yellow acrylic paints

Poppy Designs

Approach

1. Discuss the vibrant and colourful floral designs in the illustrations and compare them with Marimekko poppy designs.

2. Add a design to a section of fabric for use in a display. Use the Marimekko poppy design as a starting point. Ask the children to draw a poppy on A3 paper and go over it, pressing hard, with a felt-tip pen. Place the drawing underneath a large piece of printing cotton fabric and starting from the inside working outwards, paint the image with fabric paint. Repeat the process several times.

3. Using air-drying clay, make some poppy heads in the same style as the Marimekko poppy design. Paint and varnish using PVA glue.

4. Use the Internet to find out about Marimekko and the designer Maija Isola's interior textiles, in particular the famous poppy design (Unikko flower). Ask the children to write a magazine article about Marimekko including details of the fabric they have designed along with suggestions for its use, for example soft furnishings, cushions and fashion items.

5. Display the fabric along with some examples of Marimekko designs and with a magazine article.

6. Display the clay poppies on a piece of plain fabric with leaves cut from green paper.

Resources
- Printing cotton fabric
- A3 paper and felt pens
- Fabric paints
- Images of textile designs from Marimekko
- Air-drying clay
- Paint and PVA glue
- Green paper

Bosnia – Petar's Song

Read *Petar's Song* by Pratima Mitchell, illustrated by Caroline Binch (published by Frances Lincoln). This powerful story evokes the hardship, loneliness and fear that war brings to both children and adults. The key character, Petar, is separated from his father and forced to leave home with the rest of his family. They travel over the mountains and arrive at a strange town which is full of refugees with nowhere to stay and nothing to eat. After sleeping in a doorway on a freezing night, they are offered a garden shed as a makeshift shelter. As Christmas approaches, Petar thinks of a new song and makes up lyrics to go with the tune. The words of his song send a clear message of peace and hope for the future. The realistic illustrations reflect the sense of loneliness and isolation that refugees often endure. The details in the clothing, such as the women's head scarves, and the detailed patterns in the tablecloth are typical of those found in Bosnia. At the end of the story, Petar starts playing his violin and the townspeople start dancing jigs, polkas and waltzes joyfully.

Violin Strikes A Chord!

How many chords must a violin play, before the sound makes a tune?

How many notes must come from his heart, before he can make people laugh?

The answer my friend, is dancin' in the wind, the answer is dancin' in the wind

How many roads must a man walk down, before you call him a man?

Resources

- Violin
- Sketching pencils
- Water colours and pastels
- Cartridge paper
- Small pieces of wood
- Glue
- Acetate

Violin

Approach

1. Discuss how Petar and his family must have been feeling as they walked over the mountains carrying all they had in the world on their backs.

2. Provide a violin or some photographs of violins and discuss their shape and design. Ask the children to make observational sketches of violins.

3. Listen to a song with lyrics about peace; for example Bob Dylan's *Blowing in the Wind* and, using Petar's song as a starting point, write a new verse using the theme of peace.

4. Display the violin sketches with the songs on a background of musical notation with the notes matching the verses. Glue some pieces of wood to the back of one or two of the violin sketches to give a 3-D effect. Write the verses on acetate and place on the display. Make an eye-catching title.

The Landscape

Approach

Resources
- Watercolours
- Charcoal sticks and chalk pastels
- A3 sketch paper

1. Discuss the illustration at the beginning of the story which depicts the crumbling buildings of a village. Look at the same image at the end of the story and discuss how the use of different colours and a change of season transform the image.

2. Ask the children to write a week's diary entry from Petar's point of view which describes his feelings about having to leave his home and his father, and about his journey through familiar and unfamiliar landscapes. Alternatively, children may like to write the lyrics to a song, reflecting the feelings in the story.

3. Use the illustrations of the village scene in Winter and Spring as a starting point. Make two contrasting landscape paintings one depicting damaged buildings in a Winter setting and the other showing the same setting in Springtime. Use charcoal sticks to create the right atmosphere in the Winter scene with brown and blue watercolours. In the Spring scene, add splashes of yellow and green chalk pastels with birds in the sky. In both paintings use small sticks of wood to create a 3-D effect.

The Dance

Approach

1. Discuss the importance of dance in the story both at the beginning when Petar plays his violin and the children go through the village singing and dancing and at the end in the café when Petar picks up his violin and begins to play again. At this point, all the customers start dancing joyfully, full of hope for the future.

2. Listen to a piece of lively violin music, for example a jig, and make up a simple dance routine for the class. Take photos of the children dancing.

Resources
- Violin music CD
- Digital camera
- Black card

3. Ask the children to write a set of instructions explaining how to do the dance, using language that is clear and concise with imperative verbs.

4. Display the set of dance instructions with black cut-outs of shoes and mount on a violin-shaped piece of card.

Denmark – The Little Match Girl

Read *The Little Match Girl* from *Tales of Hans Christian Andersen* translated by Naomi Lewis, illustrated by Joel Stewart (published by Walker Books). In this thought-provoking fairy tale, the key character, a little girl, sells matches in order to survive. The story was first published in 1848 and the city of Copenhagen is the inspiration for Andersen's setting. The story opening is powerful: the little girl is described as walking the streets dressed in rags, with nothing on her feet as she has lost her slippers in the snow. It is New Year's Eve and inside the houses bright lights show people celebrating with delicious food. In contrast, the little girl is so bitterly cold that she strikes matches to keep warm. With each burning match she imagines a wonderful scene full of comfort and warmth.

Once the flame goes out, the image disappears. However, when she strikes the fourth match, the image before her becomes more lasting and appealing. Finally, she strikes all of her matches to create a brilliant glow that lights up the sky. Although the ending is very sad, the little match girl finds the peace and contentment that have eluded her in this world and hope comes out of despair. The illustrations reflect the importance of light in the story both in the night sky and in the glowing light from the matches that are extinguished all too soon.

The Street Scene

Approach

Resources
- Cardboard and black card
- Paints, pastels and pens
- Wooden spoons and pipe cleaners
- Cotton wool and glitter

1. Discuss the contrasting images in the story which portray both wealth and poverty. The little match girl, outside in freezing weather trying to sell her matches, imagines scenes of wealth and comfort. Discuss what she might be dreaming about.

2. Make a simple set for a street scene which depicts the little match girl gazing longingly through a window at the bright lights and scrumptious food within. Use cardboard to create external walls in a street and paint them. Cut out a section of one wall to make a window.

3. Create a scene through the window, including a table with food and other details within the room. Use vibrant pastels and collage materials. Add detail with gold and silver pens to create a luminous quality.

4. Display the set with the painting placed behind the window. Cut strips of black card and place in front of the window for window panes. Children could make some simple figures using wooden spoons and pipe cleaners. Scatter some white cotton wool with silver glitter for the snow.

5. Ask the children to write descriptive paragraphs to set the scene for the story. Grab the reader's attention by posing a question and setting the scene using a powerful opening line. Write in the past tense.

6. Display the descriptive writing with the street scene.

The Christmas Tree

Approach

1. Discuss how the little match girl strikes a match to keep herself warm and imagines a wonderful, glowing Christmas tree.

2. Make a large Christmas tree from thick card and cut out a silhouette tree shape. Ask children to construct the tree using green tissue paper, brown paint for the stump and decorative patterns on the pot.

3. Ask the children to make individual candles by rolling A5 paper (painted cream or pale yellow) into tubes. Stick some shiny red paper in a flame shape on top of the candles. Stick the candles on to the Christmas tree.

4. Choose one of the images that the little match girl sees in the story as a starting point for poetry writing. Ask the children to write a two-verse poem; with one verse describing how poverty affects her life and the other describing how she wishes things could be. Write in rhyming couplets using alliteration and powerful verbs to create atmosphere. Display the poems around the Christmas tree.

Resources

- A5 cartridge paper
- Shiny paper
- Poster paint
- A large piece of strong card
- Green tissue paper

My Life From The Beginning

You could never imagine my life,
It's like living on the edge of a knife,
Cold, dangerous and dark,
Not even one tiny bright spark,
Should I live or should I die?
And float right into the sky.

I will be happy of that I am sure,
For my new life will be the cure,
Up in paradise with the one that love's me,
Together I know we shall be,
Happy forever-more,
In a place that doesn't matter if you are poor.

By Ellie Fuller

The Slippers

Approach

1. Discuss how at the beginning of the story, the little match girl loses one of her slippers and how the other one is taken away. She has to walk, dressed in rags, on bare feet in the snow.

2. Ask the children to design a pair of slippers that are both warm and comfortable. Then make 3-D slippers using vibrant fabrics and wadding. Join the sections together by stitching.

3. Research on the Internet how in Victorian times poor children had to work from an early age. Discuss the sorts of jobs they did, for example chimney sweeps, and focus on their working conditions, their clothes and footwear.

4. Using information from the Internet, ask the children to write a diary entry recording a typical working day in a poor child's life. Use time sub-headings and write in the first person using a conversational tone. Illustrate with images linking to the work.

Resources

- Fabric in different colours and textures
- Wadding
- Threads and needles for stitching

England – The Mousehole Cat

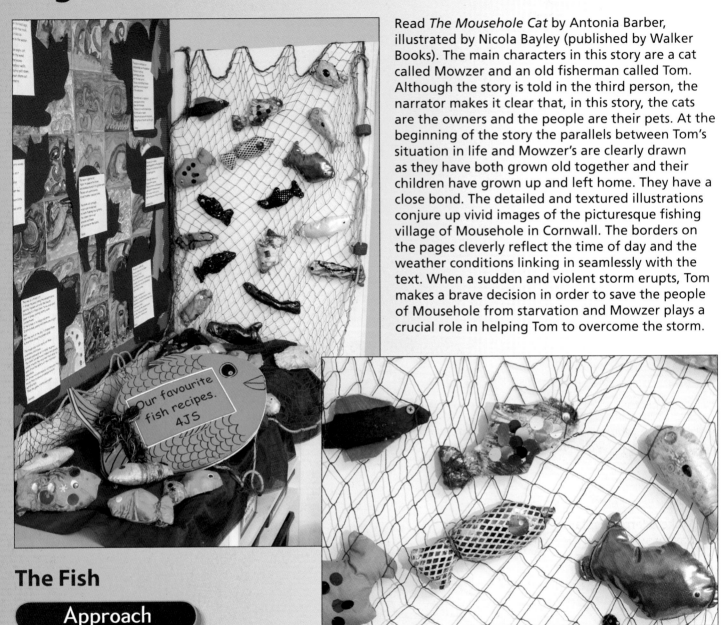

Read *The Mousehole Cat* by Antonia Barber, illustrated by Nicola Bayley (published by Walker Books). The main characters in this story are a cat called Mowzer and an old fisherman called Tom. Although the story is told in the third person, the narrator makes it clear that, in this story, the cats are the owners and the people are their pets. At the beginning of the story the parallels between Tom's situation in life and Mowzer's are clearly drawn as they have both grown old together and their children have grown up and left home. They have a close bond. The detailed and textured illustrations conjure up vivid images of the picturesque fishing village of Mousehole in Cornwall. The borders on the pages cleverly reflect the time of day and the weather conditions linking in seamlessly with the text. When a sudden and violent storm erupts, Tom makes a brave decision in order to save the people of Mousehole from starvation and Mowzer plays a crucial role in helping Tom to overcome the storm.

The Fish

Approach

1. Discuss the delicious fish dishes that Mowzer and Tom eat during the week for supper. Although they all contain fish as a basic ingredient, there is a real variety from one day to the next. Emphasise the importance of eating fish as part of a balanced, healthy diet and mention how the people of Mousehole depended on the fishermen's daily catch of fish to survive.

2. Collectively write a fish recipe for a cookery book. The recipe will need a clear title with a list of ingredients in bullet points and numbered instructions explaining how to make the dish. Use simple language, imperative verbs and write in the second person. It would be helpful to make the dish first and jot down some notes as a helpful reminder before writing the instructions.

3. Look at the illustration showing the fish that Tom caught in his nets. Focus on their silver, blue, green and mottled brown colours and their texture. Ask the children to make some 3-D fish from fabric. Embellish with sequins and shiny buttons.

4. Display the fish in a net along with the fish recipe presented in a fish-shaped cookery book.

Resources
- Netting
- Fabric, sequins and buttons
- Wadding
- Silver and blue threads

The Storm

Approach

1. Discuss how the storm is presented as a 'Great-Storm-Cat clawing his way towards the harbour'. Ask the children to look at the colours, shapes and patterns in the illustrations and then create a simple line drawing of a stormy sea, then introduce colour using pastels. Transfer the design onto a small square of cartridge paper, paint in metallic paint and then piece the squares together, like tiles, to make a large painting of a stormy sea.

2. Discuss the effects of the storm on the people in Mousehole. Ask the children to write a two verse poem. The first verse should describe the sea before the storm and the second verse should describe it during the storm. The storm should portray the image of a giant cat prowling around creating havoc.

3. Display the poems mounted on black, cat-shaped, sugar paper and use the tiles as a background.

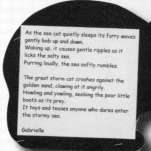

As the sea cat quietly sleeps its furry waves gently bob up and down.
Waking up, it causes gentle ripples as it licks the salty sea.
Purring loudly, the sea softly rumbles.

The great storm cat crashes against the golden sand, clawing at it angrily.
Howling and yowling, seeking the poor little boats as its prey.
It toys and teases anyone who dares enter the stormy sea.

Gabrielle

The Homecoming

Approach

1. Discuss how the people of Mousehole must have felt when they discovered that Tom's boat was missing and how they waited for him with candles and lanterns along the harbour.

2. Make a large display of Tom's homecoming. Create the scene by painting a row of cottages for the background in dark colours and placing shiny paper in the windows to represent lighted candles. Paint some boxes with sponges to create a mottled effect and place in the foreground to represent the harbour walls.

Make some stand-up people out of card and place at various places on the harbour walls. Make some lanterns by using black sugar paper or card for the outline and silver, shiny paper for the bulb and place a circle of gold paper behind it. Bend the lanterns to create a 3-D effect and stick them onto the display. Put some scrunched up paper or fabric under some white netting for waves in the foreground.

Resources

- Small squares of cartridge paper
- Metallic paints and pastels
- Black sugar paper

Resources

- Boxes
- Netting
- Paper or fabric
- Card
- Silver and gold shiny paper
- Oil pastels

Scotland – Greyfriars Bobby

Read *Greyfriars Bobby* retold and illustrated by Ruth Brown (published by Red Fox). This story is set in the city of Edinburgh. The illustrations conjure up a real sense of place and capture the beauty of the city's architecture. The main character, Bobby, is a little dog whose courage and loyalty to his master, Jock, has a powerful impact on the reader. The story begins in modern-day Edinburgh, but the reader is cleverly transported, through the illustrations, back to Victorian times when the story actually happened. Bobby is devoted to his master and when Jock dies Bobby visits the churchyard where he is buried every day and eventually makes the place his home. The obvious affection that the local people had for Bobby is uplifting and at the end of the story, the reader is told that a statue was erected in memory of Bobby's loyalty to his master. The story is all the more moving because it is a true one.

The Cityscape

Approach

1. Discuss the effectiveness of the illustrations in the story and how the architecture of Edinburgh is reflected in the pale stone buildings and the cobbled streets. Point out the castle perched high above the rest of the city.

2. Ask the children to research about Edinburgh on the Internet, in particular the part of the city called Greyfriars. Find out about the churches, museums, university buildings and the castle.

3. Children could make a collection of sketches using a variety of buildings in Edinburgh as starting points. Add detail, such as the name of the building, and any special decorative feature. Working from photographs and sketches, make 2-D clay models of a variety of buildings found in Edinburgh. Use clay tools to add detail. Place the clay buildings on a board to represent the distinctive architecture of Edinburgh.

4. Ask the children to write a tourist guide book in the form of a report. As part of the report, comment on what the buildings look like, what they are made from, the name of the architect and what they are used for.

5. Display the clay buildings and the tourist guide books with children's sketches and photographs of buildings in Edinburgh.

Resources
- Air-drying clay
- Clay tools
- Photographs of Edinburgh

The Hills

Approach

1. Discuss how Bobby and Jock used to walk for miles in the hills where Jock had lived as a small boy. Discuss the contrast between the hustle and bustle of city life and the tranquility in the surrounding hills.

2. Write a group poem which describes these contrasting landscapes.

3. Create a display showing Jock and Bobby walking amongst the rolling hills. Use different shades of green to depict the hills.

4. Write the poem on the undulating hills in the display and place Jock and Bobby in the foreground.

Resources
- Green and black sugar paper
- Watercolour paints and pastels
- Cartridge paper

Bobby

Approach

1. Discuss the things that Bobby and Jock did together in Edinburgh and how Bobby's faithfulness was rewarded. Focus on how the sort of work people did in Victorian times differed from work now. Discuss children's own pets or pets they would like to have and their importance in their lives.

2. Ask the children to create portraits of their pets using acrylic paints. Make an interesting shaped cardboard frame which represents a link between children and their pets, for example a colourful ball, a special bowl, an engraved collar or a favourite toy. Children could use photographs of themselves with their pets as a starting point.

3. Ask the children to write a short piece of descriptive writing from Bobby's perspective about the places he visited and the work he did with his master. Make sure the writing is set in Victorian times.

4. Display the portraits with the descriptive writing.

I used to walk over the hills with my companion Old Jock. The whistling of the cool wind through the trees while we walked. We were like brothers striding together while a sweet scent of summer was being carried by the wind. The long summer walks were much better than those bitter cold days. The only warmth we had during the winter months was the warmth from our friendship.

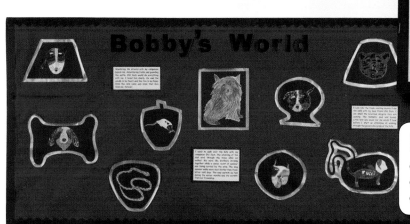

Resources
- Photographs of children and their pets
- Acrylic paints
- Card for frames and silver and gold pens

Ireland – Una and the Sea-Cloak

Read *Una and the Sea-Cloak* by Malachy Doyle, illustrated by Alison Jay (published by Frances Lincoln). This enchanting story is set by the seashore and the main character, Una, arrives after a severe storm on the beach but the magical sea-cloak she is wearing is in tatters. Luckily for Una, she meets Martin and his mother and they both look after her and try to mend her cloak. The landscape in the illustrations is very reminiscent of Ireland's coastline. A nautical theme runs throughout the story and there are many clues about the family's connection with the sea. The colour green is predominant in the story and as Ireland is often referred to as the Emerald Isle, the colour green is very evocative of the Irish landscape. The clothes worn by the characters, such as the Aran jumper and the tweed skirt, reflect a very traditional Irish costume. At the end of the story, Una rewards Martin's kindness with a special gift which holds magical powers and thus ensures that his adventures have only just begun!

The Cityscape

> **Approach**

Resources
- Watercolour paints
- Sketch paper

1. Discuss how the author uses very descriptive language and powerful verbs to create the setting for the story. There is a balance of narrative and dialogue which draws the reader in. The combination of simple, compound and complex sentences give the writing pace and makes it more interesting.

2. Look at the illustrations of the shore with details like pebbles, starfish, crabs, shells and seaweed scattered on the sandy beach. Focus on the scene where Martin first speaks to Una. Ask the children to paint a watercolour picture of a seascape with a blue, cloudy sky in the background. Divide the foreground into three sections – the sea, the sand and the cottage surrounded by cliffs. As a final touch, paint some crabs, pebbles and starfish on the sand.

3. Write an additional episode using the same style and setting.

4. Display the watercolour paintings with the children's writing.

Celebrations

Approach

1. Discuss the end of the story when Una takes Martin and his mother to her beautiful underwater palace for a great feast. As a special gift, Una gives Martin a sea-cloak so that he will be able to visit her whenever he wants. Discuss what children wear for special occasions and how they feel about celebratory events.

2. Working in small groups, show children how to knit a scarf. When the scarves are complete ask the children to decorate the scarf to make it suitable for a special occasion. Use silver threads to add sparkle and embellish with silver and green sequins, beads, feathers and ribbons.

3. Ask the children to write a short play script based on the story adding sound and music to create just the right atmosphere.

4. Display the green scarves with the play script.

Resources
- Green wool
- Threads, sequins, feathers and beads

The Search

Approach

1. Discuss the setting of the story and how the main characters' search for the silver grasses, tiny, green feathers and rare, sparkling shells took them to bog lands, mountain lakes and remote islands. Include in the discussion how these materials were used to make Una's sea-cloak.

2. Make a collaborative, large sea-cloak.

3. Ask the children to make some textile paintings which reflect the main events of the story (see page 20).

4. The children could perform the play script version of the story to an audience. Include some Irish tap dancing as part of the programme. Use the scarves and sea-cloak as part of the costumes. The textile paintings can be used as background props.

5. Design an illustrated programme for the performance which can be handed out to the audience beforehand. Include the title of the play with a synopsis of its story.

Resources
- Fabric paint
- A large piece of green or blue material
- Green, blue and silver threads
- Beads, shell shapes, sequins, buttons and wadding
- Green leaves
- Large pieces of calico

Wales – The Seal Children

Read *The Seal Children* by Jackie Morris (published by Frances Lincoln). This story is set in Wales, in a village surrounded by sea and cliffs. The main character, Huw, a fisherman, is married to a selkie (a seal that can assume human form) and they have twins named Ffion and Morlo. When a visitor arrives in the village and tells the inhabitants about a better life in the New World, the villagers decide to leave. Meanwhile, Ffion's mother and brother return to the sea people and they give Ffion a blue box full of precious pearls. The contents of the box pay for the villagers passage across the sea to America. As their ship sails out of Fishguard harbour, two seals appear in the sea. They have come to say goodbye. The place names, the setting, the characters' names, traditional costumes and the illustrations in general reflect a traditional Welsh scene. This is made all the more powerful because the village did once exist and its ruins still remain as a reminder of how things used to be.

Maes y Mynydd (Place of the Mountain)

Approach

1. Discuss the landscape in the story with the cliffs leading down to the sea and the cottages scattered around. Focus on how the villagers had to work extremely hard to survive and how most of what they earned went to their landlords.

2. Make a collaborative patchwork Welsh landscape. Using a sponge, paint the sky a light purple. Use small pieces of material to create the cliffs and the cottages. Add a washing line made from string with cut-out pieces of fabric for clothes.

Resources
- A selection of fabric
- String and sponges
- Poster paint
- Cartridge paper

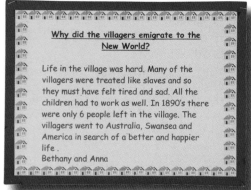

Why did the villagers emigrate to the New World?

Life in the village was hard. Many of the villagers were treated like slaves and so they must have felt tired and sad. All the children had to work as well. In 1890's there were only 6 people left in the village. The villagers went to Australia, Swansea and America in search of a better and happier life.
Bethany and Anna

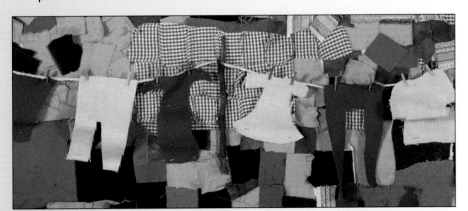

3. Ask the children to research on the Internet why people emigrated to the New World from Wales. Write a short account of this.

4. Display the writing with the collaborative landscape.

Welsh Landscapes

Approach

1. Discuss the reasons why Morlo returned to the sea people with his mother and why Ffion decided to stay. Focus on their different experiences; one living under the sea and the other leaving Fishguard harbour on the journey to the New World.

Resources
- Merino wool
- Hessian
- Collage materials

2. Make some miniature, felt Welsh landscapes using merino wool. Add some small details using the illustrations as an inspiration.

3. Brainstorm a variety of emotive words to describe the scene.

4. Display the landscapes with key words describing each scene.

The Blue Box

Approach

1. Discuss the ending of the story and how Ffion and Morlo are finally separated. Focus on the blue box that Ffion is given by her mother and brother and its significance in the story. Brainstorm some alternative endings for the story and discuss how the new endings affect the reader's view of the characters and their actions.

2. Write a class poem, using children's ideas about what they would like to put in the blue box as a treasure. Begin each verse with 'I will put in my box…'

3. Make a box that is filled with treasures from the seashore, such as shells and pebbles. Paint the box blue to reflect the colour of the sea and embellish with sequins and shiny buttons. Add detail with silver and gold pens.

4. Display the box with the class poem.

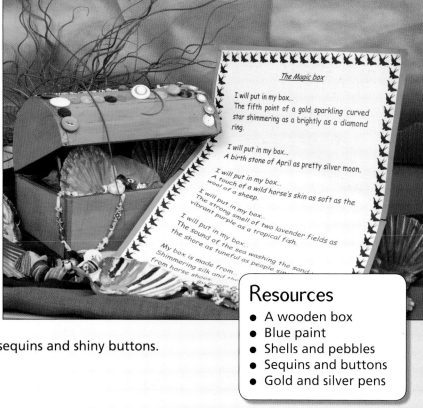

Resources
- A wooden box
- Blue paint
- Shells and pebbles
- Sequins and buttons
- Gold and silver pens

West Africa – The Fire Children

Read *The Fire Children* retold by Eric Maddern, illustrated by Frane Lessac (published by Francis Lincoln). This beautifully illustrated book is a West African folktale. It tells the story of how Nyame, the great sky god, creates the earth, the moon and the stars. One day as he looks through his trapdoor moon, admiring the earth below, he sneezes. As he does so, two spirit people, Aso Yaa and Kwaku Ananse, fall from his mouth down to the earth below. There they explore his wonderful creation and, out of loneliness, begin to make clay figures that they bake and then breathe life into creating children.

Nyame's Face

Approach

1. Discuss how Nyame's face resembles a mask and how children could make their own masks. As Nyame looked down at the two spirit people he had created, he reminded them to take care of everything he had made on the earth. Discuss why this is so important in the story.

2. Ask the children to write a description of what Nyame saw when he looked through his trapdoor down to the earth below.

3. Ask the children to make a mask of Nyame's face using a paper plate. Cut out eyes and mouth, then cover with papier mache to create features and texture. Paint and decorate.

4. Display the masks on a sky blue background.

Resources
- Paper plates
- Newspaper
- Glue
- Poster paint

Clay Children

Approach

1. Discuss why Aso Yaa and Kwaku Ananse created the clay children and the reasons for their differences.

2. Ask the children to make clay figures by rolling balls for the head and body, then adding arms and legs. Add clothes and decorate by scribing patterns using the point of a pencil. Paint when dry and glaze with PVA glue.

3. Write a set of instructions on A4 paper for making a clay figure. Attach the clay figures to a hessian board with wire. Display the set of instructions.

How to make clay 'Fire Children'

You need: clay, a board, a knife, paint and PVA glue.

- Roll some clay on a board.
- Use a knife (press lightly) to draw a child.
- Carefully cut out the child.
- Use a knife to put on a face and patterns on the clothes.
- Leave it to dry for 2 days.
- Paint it carefully.
- When dry cover with PVA glue.

Resources
- Clay
- PVA glue
- Paint
- Hessian board
- Wire

Story Scene

Approach

1. Discuss the landscape of the earth in the story and focus on its beauty. Write a list of adjectives to describe the landscape.

2. Make a textile collage of either a plant or an animal using a range of fabrics. Embellish with buttons, beads and sequins. Stitch onto hessian squares.

3. Display the textiles as a patchwork wall hanging.

Resources
- Hessian squares
- Assorted fabric
- Threads, buttons, sequins and beads

South Africa – Baba's Gift

Read *Baba's Gift* by Beverley and Maya Naidoo, illustrated by Karin Littlewood (published by Puffin). This delightful story celebrates family and kinship. Two young children, Themba and Lindi, are going to the beach and take with them their special boat made by Baba (their grandfather). On their journey through the sugar cane fields they meet a banana seller who gives them a piece of string to attach to the boat to keep it safe. On the bus to the city Themba

and Lindi sit next to a lady taking a hen to market who tells them to be careful with their boat and not to lose it. Finally at the beach, the children have great fun. They sail their boat, have a picnic, play in the sand and enjoy a game of football, but when it is time to go home their boat has disappeared! Themba and Lindi search in vain, and realising the sea has taken their boat, they find a special gift to take home for Baba. The vibrant illustrations reflect the warm climate of South Africa.

The Beach

Approach

Resources

- Cartridge paper
- Paints
- Assortment of shells
- Scissors and glue

1. Discuss the children's journey to the beach – through the sugar cane fields, on the bus over the rolling fields and finally the busy city. Compare the contrasting landscape of the countryside where they live, the busy city and the beach. Discuss the children's rising excitement as they approach their destination.

2. Compose a class poem about their journey to the beach. It could be called 'We're going to the beach'. Include the different stages of the journey, including the people met on the way. Start each verse with the line 'We're going to the beach'.

3. Perform the poem with actions and using instruments to another class.

4. Ask the children to make a painting of a beach scene and some observational drawings of shells. Cut the shells out and use to make a frame around the painted beach scene.

5. Display the poem with the paintings and photos of children using the instruments.

How would you feel if you were given a new toy boat?

We have listened to African music. Some of it made us feel happy, some of it made us feel sad.

How would you feel if you lost your new toy boat?

Resources
- Fabric
- String
- Glue
- Wooden stick
- Poster paint

Boats

Approach

1. Discuss the boat that Baba gave to Themba and Lindi – what it was made from and the type of boat. Brainstorm different types of boat and their uses.

2. Discuss with the children how they would feel if they were given a new, toy boat and how they would feel if they had lost their new, toy boat. Encourage the children to choose an appropriate facial expression to show their feelings. Take some photographs.

3. Make a large collage of a sailing boat and include either Themba and Lindi as part of the scene. Use fabric for the sails and a piece of wood for the mast of the boat.

4. Display the composition on a sea background and print boat shapes on the border. Add some group photographs and questions to the display.

Gifts

Approach

Resources
- Shiny paper
- Coloured paper
- Crayons
- Scissors

1. Discuss the gift for Baba that Themba and Lindi found on the beach, and his reaction to it.

2. Discuss the idea of invisible gifts – that do not cost anything and cannot be seen, but can be given to people by actions. For example, love, kindness, caring and friendship. Ask the children to write about a personal invisible gift and how it can be shared with others.

3. Ask the children to use shiny paper to make envelopes to hold their special gifts. Write the recipient's name on the envelope and include decoration.

4. Display the envelopes with the writing.

South Africa – The Gift of the Sun

Read *The Gift of the Sun* by Dianne Stewart, illustrated by Jude Daly (published by Frances Lincoln). In this South African tale, Thulani wants an easy life basking in the sun. When he tires of milking his cow, he sells it and buys a goat, which eats all his seeds. The goat is then exchanged for a sheep, which is then exchanged for some geese. On seeing the geese, Thulani's long-suffering wife, Dora, reminds him that they need some seeds, not geese! So the geese are exchanged for seeds. However, when the seeds grow, they are sunflowers and Dora is not very happy. But the hens feed on the sunflower seeds and begin to lay more eggs and with his new found wealth, Thulani is so busy trading animals that he has no time to laze in the sun! The small details in the quirky illustrations make this story even more appealing.

Sunflowers

Approach

1. Discuss how sunflower seeds turned out to be more profitable than Thulani and his wife Dora imagined.

2. In groups, create large sunflowers, using sunflower seeds and a selection of torn or cut yellow paper.

3. Ask the children to write a Cinquain poem about sunflowers. The first line should have one word, the second line - two words describing the colour, the third line - three words describing the size, the fourth line - four words describing the movement of the flowers following the sun and the last line with one emotive word that conjures up the image of the sunflower.

4. The poems could be displayed with the sunflowers.

Resources
- Sunflower seeds
- Selection of different types of yellow paper: crepe, tissue and gummed

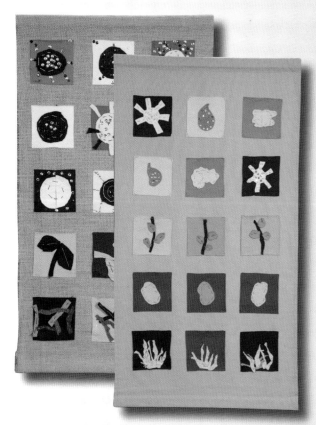

Planting and Growing

Approach

1. Discuss how, as it was Spring, Dora and Thulani decided to buy some seeds to plant their crops. Brainstorm the different types of crops that might be grown in the climate of South Africa.

2. Discuss the best conditions for growth: a temperate climate is needed for growth - in a drought, nothing will grow.

3. Make two textile collage wall hangings, one which depicts what happens to seeds planted in a climate with sun and rain and the other showing what happens in a drought. Use vivelle and felt for the component parts. For example, the seeds, cracked earth, roots, leaves, clouds, the sun and rain. Stitch on to felt squares and embellish. Arrange the squares to make the picture, placing the drought sequence on to brown hessian and the growing sequence on to green fabric.

4. Display the wall hangings side by side.

Resources
- Brown hessian and green fabric
- Felt squares
- Vivelle and felt pieces
- Threads
- Sequins
- Sunflower seeds

Thulani and Dora

Approach

1. Discuss how at the beginning of the story Thulani is rather lazy, wanting to sit in the sun all day. Point out that while Thulani is relaxing in the sun, his wife Dora is always busy – hanging the washing, picking bananas and feeding the hens. Brainstorm all the different activities of Thulani and Dora throughout the story.

2. Make two class lists, one showing all of the activities that Dora is seen to do, and the other showing all of Thulani's activities.

3. Look at the last illustration in the book, where the sun is setting and Dora and Thulani are together in front of their home, with their sunflowers and animals. Create a happy, vibrant scene of this using a variety of materials.

4. Display the lists together on the display.

Resources
- A selection of collage materials

Nigeria – Spider and the Crows

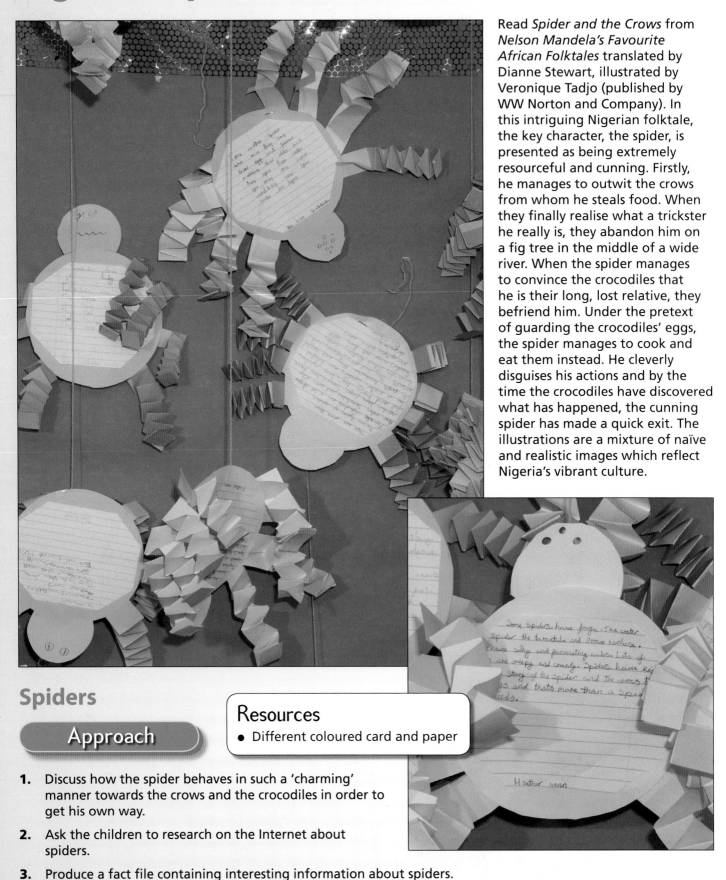

Read *Spider and the Crows* from *Nelson Mandela's Favourite African Folktales* translated by Dianne Stewart, illustrated by Veronique Tadjo (published by WW Norton and Company). In this intriguing Nigerian folktale, the key character, the spider, is presented as being extremely resourceful and cunning. Firstly, he manages to outwit the crows from whom he steals food. When they finally realise what a trickster he really is, they abandon him on a fig tree in the middle of a wide river. When the spider manages to convince the crocodiles that he is their long, lost relative, they befriend him. Under the pretext of guarding the crocodiles' eggs, the spider manages to cook and eat them instead. He cleverly disguises his actions and by the time the crocodiles have discovered what has happened, the cunning spider has made a quick exit. The illustrations are a mixture of naïve and realistic images which reflect Nigeria's vibrant culture.

Spiders

Approach

Resources
- Different coloured card and paper

1. Discuss how the spider behaves in such a 'charming' manner towards the crows and the crocodiles in order to get his own way.

2. Ask the children to research on the Internet about spiders.

3. Produce a fact file containing interesting information about spiders.

4. Display the fact files mounted on spider-shaped paper. Create legs by using concertinaed pieces of paper.

The Crows' Flight

Approach

1. Discuss all the things that the crows saw as they flew great distances to reach the fig tree.

2. Discuss what other images the crows might have seen when travelling across Nigeria and other African countries. For example, the different animals, people and physical features like rivers and mountains.

3. Ask the children to create pictures showing images of Africa. Draw the outline of the chosen images – they could be animals, flowers or even symbols – on black sugar paper and cut out as silhouettes. Place on a square of paper and add a black frame. Using wax crayons colour in the background in bright colours. Tape the framed pictures together to form a quilt effect and glaze over with PVA glue.

4. Display as a wall hanging.

Resources
- Black sugar paper
- Wax crayons
- Masking tape
- PVA glue

The Wide River

Approach

1. Discuss how the spider could have tricked the crocodiles in other ways.

2. Draw some large outlines of crocodiles and some fish-shaped outlines with a dark, thick sketch pencil. Draw in the different patterns as seen on the illustration. Choose a selection of brightly-coloured paper or card and cut out sections to match the shapes and patterns drawn on the crocodile. Stick these sections onto the body of the crocodiles and fish. Add detail with sequins. Create a spider in the same way.

3. Use coloured paper to create a background consisting of sky, land and water. Cut out a tree and leaves. Make crows from black and white paper to place on the tree.

4. Ask the children to write an additional episode for the story in which the cunning spider is finally outwitted by one of the other animals. Write in the same style as the story using the past tense and the third person with some direct speech. Use a variety of sentence structures and a range of punctuation to create a dramatic effect. Add a selection of writing to the display.

Resources
- Gummed paper in an assortment of colours
- Brightly coloured paper and card
- Sequins

Morocco – The Bachelor and the Bean

Read *The Bachelor and the Bean* retold and illustrated by Shelley Fowles (published by Frances Lincoln). In this Jewish-Moroccan tale, a grumpy old bachelor loses his last lunchtime bean down a well. Hearing his yelling, an imp jumps out of the well and gives the bachelor a magic pot to stop his noise! The pot then conjures up the most delicious food until a jealous old lady steals it. The bachelor revisits the well and is given another pot which is even better than the first one, but the old lady steals that one too. Once more the bachelor returns to the well and this time the imp gives him a pot which proves to be quite different and the bachelor's life is never the same again! The amusing illustrations are rich in detail and pattern, which is a recurring theme in this book.

Pattern

Approach

1. Discuss how pattern features throughout the illustrations of the story – in the border on the front cover, the characters' clothes and in the background.

2. Design and make a costume for one of the main characters of the story – either the grumpy old bachelor or the old lady. Use a paper pattern for the basic shape, cut out the fabric and decorate using felt pen and embellish with ribbon, sequins and buttons. Stitch the two pieces together using embroidery thread.

Resources
- Calico or similar type of plain fabric
- Felt pens
- Needles and embroidery threads
- Scissors
- Sequins, ribbon and buttons
- Tissue paper and polystyrene balls
- Thin card

3. Ask the children to write a description of the costume made. Including as much detail as possible of the colours and the pattern used.

4. Make a 3-D model of one of the characters using a semi-circle of thin card. Decorate with a pattern and make into a cone shape for the body. Attach a head made out of scrunched-up paper or a polystyrene ball, covered with tissue paper. Draw or paint on a face, then add hair and headwear.

5. Display the costumes with the descriptive pieces.

The Magic Pot

Approach

1. Discuss the pots that the imp gave to the bachelor and what came out of them – the delicious food and the vessels and plates of gold, silver and crystal.

2. Brainstorm what else could come out of a magic pot, for example, clothes, toys, games or jewellery. Make a list of possible items and mount on a piece of sugar paper cut in the shape of a pot.

3. Ask each child to make a magic pot out of clay. Paint and decorate, then glaze with PVA glue.

4. Display the clay pots with the class list.

Resources
- Sugar paper in a variety of colours
- Modelling clay
- Paint
- PVA glue

What do you think could come out of the magic pot?

a frog · cod and chips · a baby · winter leaves · paper and crayons for drawing loads of pictures · and daddy longlegs · a penguin's house · a diamond cat · a rainbow caterpillar · peacock feathers · and friend to play with me · a table · a pink butterfly · a princess · magic beans · a motorbike · a purple flower · beautiful birds

Our pots are made from clay.

Look at the Moroccan patterns that we have used to decorate them.

Resources
- Assortment of empty boxes
- Thin card
- Masking tape and glue
- Paint

The sun can be bright and hot in Morocco.

Buildings and Architecture

Approach

1. Discuss the style of architecture in Morocco as depicted in the illustrations. In this story the buildings are highly decorative, with arches, domed roofs and patterned floor tiles.

2. Compare and contrast the features of buildings in Morocco with those where the children live. Create a list under the headings of 'Morocco' and 'Own locality'.

3. Make a large collage of a Moroccan town. Make 3-D buildings from boxes, paint and decorate. Join the buildings with arches cut out of card. Place models of the characters in front of the collage together with the costumes. Construct a border for the display using a repeating pattern.

Egypt – The Day of Ahmed's Secret

The Desert | The City | The River

Read *The Day of Ahmed's Secret* by Florence Parry Heide and Judith Gilliland, illustrated by Ted Lewin (published by Puffin Books). This story is set in the ancient city of Cairo with the desert on one side and the River Nile on the other. The main character, Ahmed, is a young boy who has a special secret to tell his family but he must wait until his day's chores are completed. He rides around the city on a donkey and cart delivering very heavy canisters of butane gas for customers with gas stoves. The colourful illustrations conjure up the hustle and bustle of street life with market stalls, camels, traders with colourful carts selling food, people carrying baskets on their heads – a busy scene teaming with life. In contrast, the peaceful view of the pyramids reflects a different sense of time and place. At the end of the story, when Ahmed's secret is finally revealed, it is all the more touching because of its unexpected simplicity.

Contrasting Landscapes

Approach

Resources
- Poster paints
- Card
- Tissue paper and shiny blue paper
- Sand

1. Discuss the different landscapes found in Cairo and in particular the impact the River Nile has on its surroundings.

2. Make a collaborative painting which reflects the three main areas of the city and its setting. Divide the painting into three sections. The first section should depict the desert and the pyramids, using sand and paint to create the desert effect. The middle section should depict the bustling city scene with ancient buildings in the background and figures stuck on in the foreground as a collage. The third section should depict the river Nile with shiny blue paper for the river and green tissue paper for the reeds.

3. Brainstorm the sounds of the city: bells ringing, cars hooting, whistles blowing and the sound of Ahmed's cart. Choose some instruments to create a cacophony of sound and practise linking movement with sound. Children could mime weaving in and out within a crowded city, carrying baskets on their heads or selling fruit at the market stalls.

4. Read the story aloud to an audience and bring it to life by including the sound and movement sequences as part of the performance.

Weaving

Approach

1. Discuss the decorative patterns in the windows, on the plates and on the buildings all over the city, as illustrated in the book.

2. Look at the blankets the camels are wearing and discuss the vibrant colours that have been used.

3. Discuss the importance of the use of colour in the design process and ask children to talk about their favourite colours. Make a weaving of a simple blanket using strips of fabric with a combination of Ahmed's favourite good-luck colours: blue, green and gold.

Resources
- Strips of fabric for weaving
- Soft netting as a base for weaving

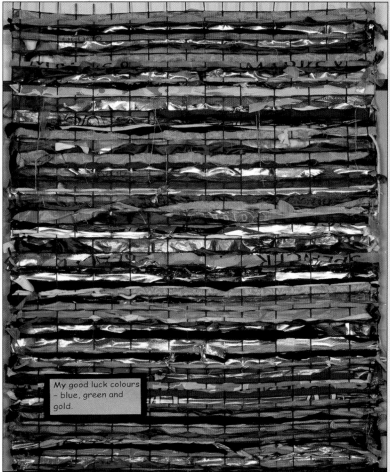

My good luck colours – blue, green and gold.

My secret is that I have a place in my bedroom – a secret place with my best toys, some sweets and my favourite books. I think I will let my best friend see this place.

Architecture

Approach

1. Discuss Egyptian buildings with their elaborate designs on the arched doorways, the ornate stone carvings and the dome-shaped roofs.

2. Cut out a large archway shape from a piece of card. Fold A5 cartridge paper in half and ask children to make individual detailed sketches of the different types of buildings in the story.

3. Discuss Ahmed's secret in the story and link to children's own special secrets. Ask the children to write a secret for each card; they could be about things children would like to achieve in the future.

4. Display the sketches on the archway, along with the hidden secrets placed inside.

Resources
- Cardboard
- Cartridge paper
- Sketch pencils
- Gold and silver pens

West Africa – The Leopard's Drum

Read *The Leopard's Drum* written and illustrated by Jessica Souhami (published by Frances Lincoln). This traditional tale from West Africa tells how a very small tortoise outwits Osebo, the proud, boastful leopard. Osebo has a magnificent drum which he plays every day and is the envy of all the animals. They all want it, but Osebo will not let anyone else have it, not even Nyame the sky god. So Nyame offers a big reward to the animal that brings him the drum. The animals all fail in their attempts to get the drum and are very dismissive of Achi-cheri, the tiny tortoise. However, he is the one who not only gets the drum, but teaches the proud and boastful leopard a lesson. The colourful and highly decorative illustrations are a feature of this story.

Resources

- Various types of drum
- Cartridge paper
- Sketching pencils, charcoal and pastels

Drums

Approach

1. Discuss Osebo's magnificent drum and the types of music that can be played on drums. Discuss musical vocabulary associated with drums, for example, rhythm, beat, loud and soft.

2. Each child could make observational sketches of African drums. Encourage them to focus on the patterns used in their designs.

3. Ask the children to write a piece of performance poetry or rap poem and link it to music, especially to drums. Base the poetry on one of the themes of the story and illustrate.

4. Perform this poetry with the music to an audience from another class.

5. Display a selection of drums with the illustrated poetry and the observational sketches.

Patterns

Approach

1. Discuss the use of pattern in the illustrations. The inside cover of the book is patterned, the illustrations of the animals feature different patterns – zig-zags, stripes and spots, and the foliage has different shapes and patterns.

2. Discuss the pattern in the story – one by one, the animals all take turns to try to get the drum for Nyame the sky god.

3. Make a storyboard of line drawings featuring the main events of the story. Using this, ask the children to write the story in their own words, with a particular focus on the beginning, making it really effective.

4. Looking at the patterns in the illustrations, children could produce individual collage tiles depicting these patterns (see page 36).

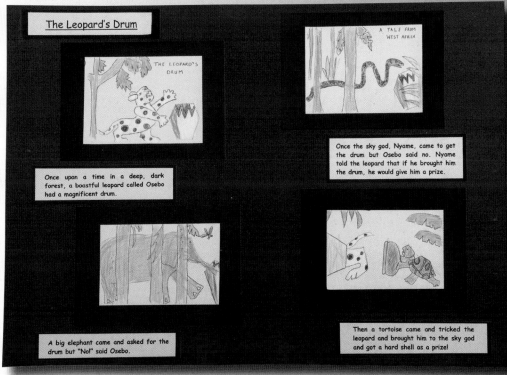

The Leopard's Drum

A TALE FROM WEST AFRICA

THE LEOPARD'S DRUM

Once upon a time in a deep, dark forest, a boastful leopard called Osebo had a magnificent drum.

Once the sky god, Nyame, came to get the drum but Osebo said no. Nyame told the leopard that if he brought him the drum, he would give him a prize.

A big elephant came and asked for the drum but "No!" said Osebo.

Then a tortoise came and tricked the leopard and brought him to the sky god and got a hard shell as a prize!

Resources
- A3 paper
- A variety of collage materials
- Scissors and glue

Rewards

Approach

1. Discuss how Achi-cheri, the tortoise, chooses a hard shell to protect her from the fierce animals as her reward from Nyame for getting him Osebo's drum.

2. Discuss what else could Achi-cheri could have chosen as a reward, perhaps a different feature or characteristic, or even a different colour.

3. Make a large model of Achi-cheri with her hard shell. Use a chicken wire base and cover with papier mache or modroc. Paint and glaze with varnish or PVA glue.

4. Write a list of instructions for making the tortoise using the imperative (placing the verb at the beginning of the sentence) and bullet points.

5. Make some birds of paradise and butterflies using different coloured card with sequins to embellish.

6. Mount the writing on green paper or card and display with the model tortoise, butterflies, and the birds of paradise.

Resources
- Chicken wire
- Papier mache or modroc
- Paint
- PVA glue or varnish
- Thin card
- Sequins

Russia – Masha and the Firebird

Read *Masha and the Firebird* by Margaret Bateson Hill, illustrated by Anne Wilson (published by Zero to Ten). This book tells the story of Masha, a young peasant girl, who lives on the edge of a forest with her mother who sells eggs at the market and her father who is a woodcutter. Masha loves to paint the smooth shells of the hens' eggs. One day while the paint is drying, she runs off into the forest to play. There she meets the magical Firebird, guardian of the eggs of the four elements – earth, water, air and fire. He asks Masha to help him hide the eggs from the witch Baba Yaga by painting them. Masha does as he asks and the first three eggs are safely hidden, but Baba Yaga manages to get her hands on the final egg. Masha then sets off on a magical adventure to find the egg and finally comes face to face with the fearsome old witch Baba Yaga.

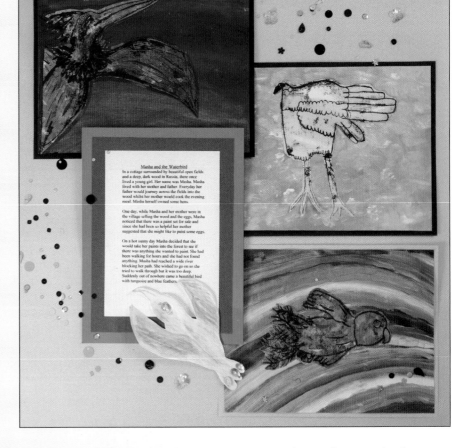

Magical Powers

Approach

1. Discuss the story with an emphasis on the plot and character development. Examine the author's style, for example, the writing is in the past tense, the use of time connectives at the beginnings of paragraphs and the balance of narrative and dialogue. The narrative is highly descriptive and uses emotive language.

2. Ask the children to make a sketch of a magical bird by combining features of different birds and think of a special power for the bird, for example, a peace bird that creates peace.

3. Children can then make a mono print of the bird by painting two sheets of A3 paper using acrylic paint – one colour for the background to symbolise the bird's power, and the other to be the colour of the bird (a contrast). On a sheet of Perspex (or the table top), roll over with black ink. Blot the surplus off with newspaper. Then place the second painted sheet (the bird's colour), face down on the black ink and using a paintbrush or finger, draw the shape of the bird on the back. Cut around the shape and mount on the first colour (background).

4. Ask the children to write an extended folktale which uses the theme of good overcoming evil as identified in *Masha and the Firebird*. The children could set the story in a Russian forest, but instead of the Firebird character, use the painted birds that they have designed as inspiration for their stories. Encourage them to focus on the bird's special powers to create an exciting plot. Write the story in the third person and include some dialogue.

5. Display the stories next to the mono prints.

Resources
- A3 paper
- Acrylic paint
- Perspex
- Newspaper
- Printing ink

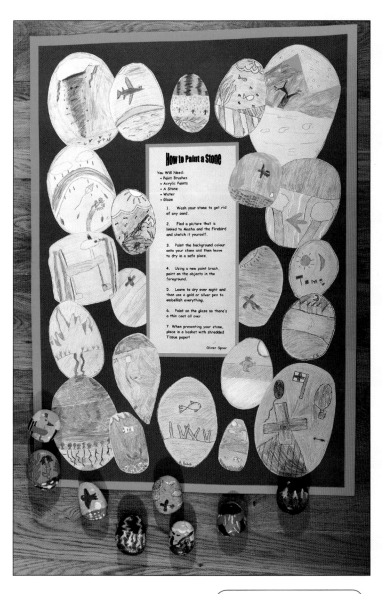

Story Pebbles

Approach

1. Discuss the significance of the four decorated eggs in the story. Look at photographs or paintings of Fabergé eggs; discuss the way they are decorated with gold and jewels and how precious they are.

2. Look at the illustrations of decorated eggs in the story and how they represent the four elements. On a smooth, egg-shaped pebble, ask children to draw the outline of a scene from their story writing, paint and decorate it with acrylic paint. Use gold and silver pens to highlight some of the features to make it more special. When dry, glaze with varnish or PVA glue.

3. Write a piece of instruction writing about how the pebbles were decorated including suggestions for display. Write in the present tense using the imperative form of the verb at the beginning of each line. Include a list of resources needed.

4. Display the decorated pebbles together with the instructions.

Resources
- Pebbles
- Acrylic paint
- Varnish or PVA glue
- Thin card
- Gold and silver pens

Bird Characters

Approach

Resources
- Clay
- Modelling tools

1. Look at the children's mono prints of birds and discuss the special powers and qualities they have been given and the colours used in their designs.

2. Make a clay bird relief using the children's sketches as a starting point. Build up layers to create a 3-D effect and use a modelling tool to add detail.

3. Read the four line poem at the end of the book and discuss its use of rhyming couplets: AA, BB. Using the same rhyming pattern, ask the children to write a poem about the character of their bird.

4. Display a selection of the clay birds with the poetry.

China – The Elephant's Pillow

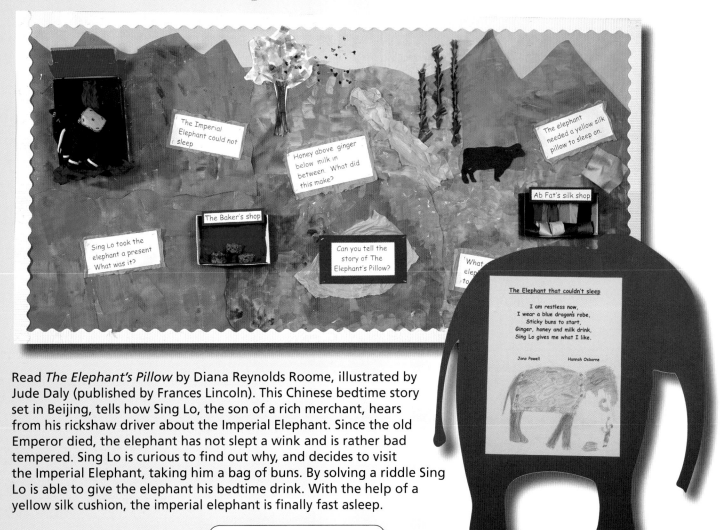

Read *The Elephant's Pillow* by Diana Reynolds Roome, illustrated by Jude Daly (published by Frances Lincoln). This Chinese bedtime story set in Beijing, tells how Sing Lo, the son of a rich merchant, hears from his rickshaw driver about the Imperial Elephant. Since the old Emperor died, the elephant has not slept a wink and is rather bad tempered. Sing Lo is curious to find out why, and decides to visit the Imperial Elephant, taking him a bag of buns. By solving a riddle Sing Lo is able to give the elephant his bedtime drink. With the help of a yellow silk cushion, the imperial elephant is finally fast asleep.

The Elephant

Approach

Resources
- Cardboard boxes
- Poster paint
- Plastic flower pots
- Calico and fabric paints
- A2 card

1. Discuss what an elephant looks like in terms of size, colour and shape. Refer to the illustrations in the story.

2. Make a very large elephant using cardboard boxes for the head and body and plastic flower pots for the legs. Cover the structure using thick paper and paint it grey.

3. Design and make a colourful cloth to drape over the elephant.

4. Write a Tanka poem which describes the appearance and character of the elephant in this story. A Tanka is a Japanese form of poetry and has five lines and thirty-one syllables used in the following way: 5, 7, 5, 7 and 7. As in Haiku and Cinquains, every word is important and must be chosen carefully.

The Pillow

1. Discuss how the elephant needed the yellow silk cushion to be comfortable at bedtime.

2. Create an abstract design for a pillow or cushion using fabric paint and a large piece of fabric.

3. Display the fabric with wadding behind it to create a 3-D cushion or pillow for the imperial elephant

4. Look at the final display and brainstorm words that describe its visual impact.

Resources
- Fabric paint
- Large piece of cotton fabric
- Wadding

Bedtime Routines

1. Discuss how the Imperial Elephant could not sleep without his bedtime routine, which included his special drink and something comfortable to lie on.

2. Discuss with the children what they like to have with them and what they do before they go to sleep. Illustrate with drawings of themselves at bedtime and add captions.

3. Ask the children to paint a picture of themselves at bedtime.

4. Display the paintings with captions.

Resources
- Cartridge paper
- Crayons and oil pastels
- Collage materials
- Buttons, beads and sequins

China – Aladdin

Read *Aladdin* retold by Philip Pullman, illustrated by Sophy Williams (published by Scholastic Press). This delightful story is full of magic and excitement. It tells the tale of Aladdin, an idle and selfish boy, who discovers an enchanted lamp. On his adventures, he finds some fruit which turns into precious sparkling jewels which he uses to win the Sultan's daughter in marriage. Towards the end of the story, Aladdin abandons his idle ways and becomes both a wealthy and a wise man, but he has many obstacles to overcome before he finds true happiness. Although the setting is in China, the richly coloured and exotic illustrations are reminiscent of Arabian countries.

The Enchanted Lamp

Approach

1. Discuss the lamp and ask the children each to write down three wishes.

2. Ask the children to paint enchanted lamps. These could be decorated with 3-D sparkling jewels. Display the children's wishes with the lamps.

3. Ask the children each to write a concrete poem describing a precious jewel. In concrete poetry the layout of the words represents the subject matter. Cut out the poems and mount on 'cushions'.

Resources

- Oil pastels
- Beads and plastic jewels
- Cartridge paper
- Coloured paper
- Fabric and padding

The Sorcerer and Badr al-Budur

Approach

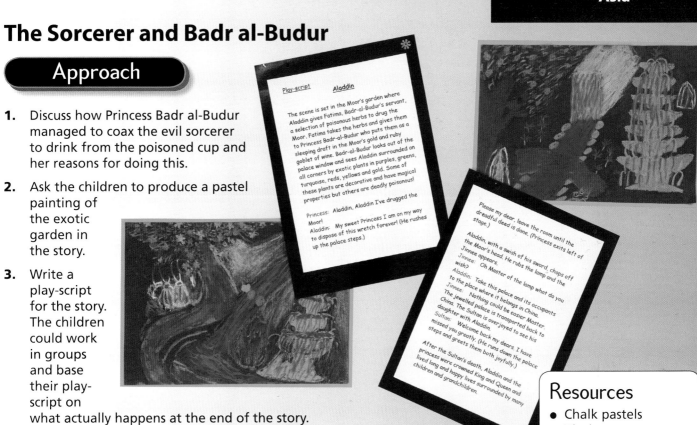

1. Discuss how Princess Badr al-Budur managed to coax the evil sorcerer to drink from the poisoned cup and her reasons for doing this.

2. Ask the children to produce a pastel painting of the exotic garden in the story.

3. Write a play-script for the story. The children could work in groups and base their play-script on what actually happens at the end of the story. Include stage directions and describe the exotic setting at the beginning of the scene to create the right mood.

Resources
- Chalk pastels
- Black sugar paper
- Gold and silver pens

The Night Sky

Approach

1. Discuss how the shapes and colours of the buildings in the story reflect a different culture.

2. Ask the children to make watercolour paintings of the night sky showing dome-shaped buildings. Paint the moon, stars and lights with metallic acrylic paints.

3. Children could write a description of the palace at night with the glittering lights and dome like buildings.

4. Ask the children to use non-fiction books to research the different types of buildings in Arabian countries.

5. Display the writing along with the night sky paintings.

Resources
- Watercolour paints
- Metallic acrylic paints

Hong Kong – Chopsticks

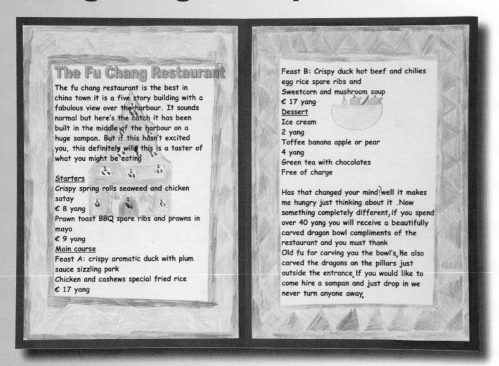

The Fu Chang Restaurant

The fu chang restaurant is the best in china town it is a five story building with a fabulous view over the harbour. It sounds normal but here's the catch it has been built in the middle of the harbour on a huge sampan. But if this hasn't excited you, this definitely will, this is a taster of what you might be eating

Starters
Crispy spring rolls seaweed and chicken satay
€ 8 yang
Prawn toast BBQ spare ribs and prawns in mayo
€ 9 yang
Main course
Feast A: crispy aromatic duck with plum sauce sizzling pork
Chicken and cashews special fried rice
€ 17 yang

Feast B: Crispy duck hot beef and chilies egg rice spare ribs and
Sweetcorn and mushroom soup
€ 17 yang
Dessert
Ice cream
2 yang
Toffee banana apple or pear
4 yang
Green tea with chocolates
Free of charge

Has that changed your mind? well it makes me hungry just thinking about it. Now something completely different, if you spend over 40 yang you will receive a beautifully carved dragon bowl compliments of the restaurant and you must thank Old fu for carving you the bowl's. He also carved the dragons on the pillars just outside the entrance. If you would like to come hire a sampan and just drop in we never turn anyone away.

Read *Chopsticks* by Jon Berkeley (published by Oxford University Press). This magical story is set in Hong Kong and the vivid illustrations reflect its rich culture. The images of the floating restaurant and its menu, the contrasting landscapes, and even the main character's name, Chopsticks, depict powerful images of China. Chopsticks, a small grey mouse, lives in the floating restaurant and he is intrigued when a carved wooden dragon, which is coiled around one of the pillars at the entrance to the floating restaurant, starts whispering to him. The wooden dragon tells Chopsticks about the special woodcarver, Old Fu, who made him and he urges Chopsticks to visit him and discover the magic that will enable him to fly. Towards the end of the story, Chopsticks and the wooden dragon start having wonderful adventures together soaring through the sky. However, they make sure that Old Fu is not forgotten.

Views from Above

Approach

1. Towards the end of the story, the illustrations depict some aerial shots of the places Chopsticks and the dragon fly over during their exciting journey. Discuss how views from above give a totally different perspective to a setting. Look at photographs of aerial views and especially the work of the photographer Yann Arthus-Bertrand and focus on his use of colour.

2. Ask children to imagine a special journey and to plot out the route from above (a bird's eye view). Using Yann Arthus-Bertrand's style, ask children to draw an aerial view of their journey in a sketch book. Choose a section of the drawing and transfer the image onto A3 sketch paper. Use chalk pastels in the same colours chosen by Yann Arthus-Betrand.

3. Transfer the image to calico and paint it with fabric paints and dyes. Place wadding underneath and sandwich together with another piece of calico. Sew the sides together and using a variety of coloured threads, pick out parts of the detail with stitching.

4. Ask the children to write an advertisement for a local newspaper which entices readers to book a table at a floating Chinese restaurant. Include a sample menu with an eye-catching heading and write in the second person. Use emotive language, in particular tempting and positive words, to enhance what the restaurant has on offer.

Resources
- A3 paper
- Calico
- Fabric paint and dyes
- Different coloured embroidery threads
- Wadding
- Chalk pastels

Chinese Lanterns

Approach

1. Look at Chinese artefacts, paintings and writing and discuss in terms of colour, shape and texture.

2. Use the illustrations of Chinese lanterns in the story as a starting point. Cut out the centre of a piece of A4 card so that only the frame is left. Place white tissue paper over both sides and glue with an equal mixture of PVA glue and water. Look at different curved shapes in the illustrations and cut out or use torn pieces of tissue paper in pinks and reds to create a contrast. Glue on top of the white tissue paper. Make four of these. Place some Chinese writing or an outline of a dragon using black ink pens on top of the layers of tissue paper. Paint over the frames and attach the four sides together to make a lantern. Stick tassels or beads on the end of the lantern and hang at different levels.

3. Ask the children to write a brief prequel to the story using the author's style. The language used is simple but effective, combining narrative and some dialogue. Towards the end of the story, personification is used to create a more vivid image of the scene. Focus on how the character of Old Fu came to make such a special dragon even though he was almost blind at the time. Write the prequel so that the ending leads seamlessly into the rest of the story. The children could read the prequel to the class.

Resources

- A4 card and black ink pens
- Poster paint, tassels and beads
- Tissue paper in white, pink and red

Dragon Model

Approach

1. Look at illustrations of dragons and discuss their appearance in terms of colour and shape. Focus on the dragon in the story.

2. Collectively, make a papier mache dragon. Paint it using vibrant colours.

3. Write group poems about the dragon in the story. Focus on the dragon's qualities, for example gentleness, the gift of speech and a willingness to share adventures. Put the title Carved Dragon on a piece of paper and circulate it around the group so everyone has a chance to add a line. Different styles can add to the texture of the poems and can also lead to exciting developments. Figurative language – alliteration, simile and onomatopoeia will increase the impact and create mood.

4. Display the 3-D dragon model with the poem.

Carved Dragon

Coiled, carved and calm
Observing life's hustle and bustle.
Wooden whispers spring to life,
About Old Fu his creator.
Taking Chopsticks on a journey,
Soaring through the sky
Like a dancing kite.
A dragon's eye view of the world.

Resources

- Poster paints
- Papier mache materials

India – Monkey-See, Monkey-Do

Read *Monkey-See, Monkey-Do* from *The Story Tree: Tales to Read Aloud* retold by Hugh Lupton, illustrated by Sophie Fatus (published by Barefoot Books). This amusing story is about a hat seller who is wheeling his cart full of hats through the jungle when disaster strikes. One of the wheels of his cart gets stuck in a hole in the road and the cart tips over. As the hats spill on to the road, hundreds of monkeys swing down from the trees and take all the hats. When the man shouts at the monkeys to give him back his hats, they shout back and they then copy all of his actions. At last, in exasperation, the man throws his hat to the ground and picks up his cart and starts to push it along the road. As he does so, the monkeys copy him and throw all their hats down on to the ground so the man is able to continue on his way to the market. The illustrations depict the man's journey through the jungle.

Hats

Approach

1. Discuss the variety of hats the man has on his cart. Brainstorm other types of hat, including those from other countries.

2. Ask the children to design a hat, basing their design on who will wear it. For example, a hat for a gardener could have a design with a pattern of flowers or garden tools and a hat for a mechanic could have a spanner detail on it.

3. Using an assortment of materials, make the hat according to the design.

4. Ask the children to write a short piece to say who the hat is for and how the design reflects this.

5. Make a large collage scene of the monkeys throwing the hats out of the trees and display the writing with it.

Resources
- Assorted fabrics and materials
- Scissors and glue
- Sequins and buttons
- Collage materials

Carts

Approach

1. Discuss how in India people use carts, bicycles and old vehicles to carry their goods to sell in the villages and at markets.

2. Look at the man's cart in the story – the design, the pattern and decoration.

3. Ask the children to make 3-D carts using cardboard boxes. Attach handles using lolly sticks or art straws and wheels made from card circles with straw spokes. Paint and decorate with colourful patterns.

4. Make a label for the cart and a list of all the items for sale. For example, the cart could sell items of clothing, shoes, fruit or hardware.

5. Display the models with the labels and lists.

Resources
- Cardboard boxes of varying sizes
- Scissors and glue
- Art straws or lolly sticks
- Card
- Paint

A Fabric Indian Truck

Resources
- Piece of calico or print cotton
- Fabric paints
- Gold paint

Approach

1. Explain that in India trucks are used to sell silks, threads, powdered paint and spices. The trucks are often extremely colourful and beautifully painted.

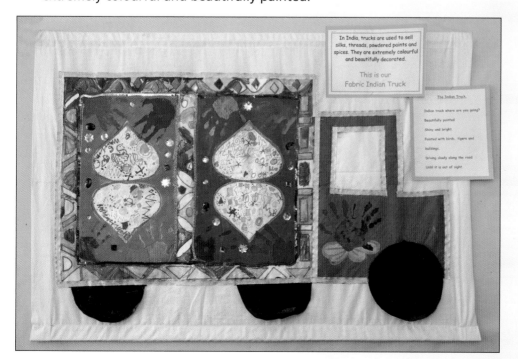

2. Collectively, make a fabric Indian truck. Draw an outline of the truck on a piece of calico or print cotton. Divide the truck into sections and using fabric paint, draw on patterns and images of India in each section. Outline each section in gold paint.

3. Make a class or a group poem describing the truck – its appearance, where it is going and what it is selling.

4. Display the fabric truck with the poem.

India – The Tiger Child

Read *The Tiger Child* retold and illustrated by Joanna Troughton (published by Puffin). In this folk tale, the main character is a tiger who is faced with a dilemma. He has lost the fire that cooks his food and has to visit the village to reclaim it. When he arrives at the village, the people are so frightened of the tiger that he is unable to get close enough to them to ask for the fire. The tiger decides to send his nephew, a tiger cub, to the village instead. When the tiger child arrives he is treated with such kindness and is pampered so much that he forgets what he was sent for in the first place. The colourful illustrations reflect the colours of India and its designs.

The Tiger

Approach

Resources
- Collage materials
- Corrugated card
- A selection of green, yellow and black sugar paper

1. Discuss the character of the tiger in the story and his reasons for sending his nephew to visit the village.

2. Look at the illustration in the story where the tiger is cooking his food with the other animals watching him. Discuss the striking patterns and colours in the picture.

3. Create a collage display which includes most of the animals in the story with the tiger as the focal point in the centre. Make a green background from frieze paper and build up a canopy of leaves in greens and yellows. Make some larger leaves from different shades of green sugar paper with veins painted on them and place them on the middle of the display with monkeys' heads and tails peeping up between the leaves. In the foreground, put some yellow sugar paper on the display and cover with corrugated card painted green and cut to represent the high grass. Place a selection of animals made from collage materials on the display and in the centre place the tiger peering out through the leaves.

4. The children could use the Internet to research information about tigers in India. Write in the present tense and in the third person. Present the writing in the form of an information leaflet.

5. Display the animal collage with the information leaflets.

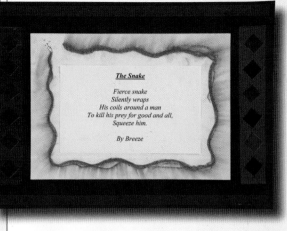

The Snake

The Snake

Fierce snake
Silently wraps
His coils around a man
To kill his prey for good and all,
Squeeze him.

By Breeze

Resources

- Pen and waterproof ink
- Watercolour paints and paper
- Materials for batik work

Approach

1. Look at the illustrations of the animals in the story and their surroundings. Focus on the snake, its pattern and colour.

2. Ask the children to make a pen and ink drawing of the snake on watercolour paper. Use watercolour paints to add colour.

3. Create a vibrant pattern for the snake and make a snake design. Using the pen and ink drawing as a starting point, make a batik which features the snake.

4. Ask the children to write a cinquain poem which focuses on the colours and pattern of the snake. A cinquain is a poem which has five lines of twenty-two syllables: 2, 4, 6, 8 and 2. The last line needs to create impact and, in this case, should capture the characteristics of the snake. The lines can run into each other to be more effective. Use onomatopoeia and alliteration to create a vivid image.

Costume

Approach

Resources

- Black wool
- Beads and buttons
- Colourful fabric
- Acrylic paint
- Silver and gold paper

We made our sari with paint and exotic coloured fabrics.

Our jewellery was made from beads, string and wire.

1. Look at a variety of Indian artefacts, textiles and crafts. Discuss the saris and jewellery shown in *The Tiger Child*.

2. Make a display using a selection of collage materials depicting an Indian girl wearing a sari. Make a necklace from beads or buttons. Place some vibrant fabric around the girl to be worn as a sari.

3. The children could write a set of labels which explain the different parts of the girl's costume and jewellery.

4. Display the collage on a painted background which reflects the setting of the story and include the detailed labels.

India – One, Two, Tree!

Read *One, Two, Tree!* by Anushka Ravishankar and Sirish Rao, illustrated by Durga Bai (published by Tara Publishing). The illustrations in this book are cleverly presented as a series of detailed line drawings of animals. The drawings are closely linked to the text. Animals are introduced on the first page in bold colours and then, on the next page, the animals are placed on the tree and merge into the background. Throughout the book, both numbers and adjectives are reinforced in the text and in the quirky drawings. The animals that appear in the illustrations do not normally live in the treetops and although they are all quite different from each other, they fit on the tree together happily. As the number of animals increases, the ever-expanding tree seems to accommodate them and appears to welcome all new arrivals with open arms!

The Tree

Approach

Resources
- Different shades of green tissue paper
- PVA glue
- Black thread
- Book of nursery rhymes

1. Discuss the story with the children and use local resources, such as a woodland setting, as an inspiration for artwork.

2. Take children outside to look at trees and focus on line patterns on the trunks, branches and leaves. Develop further by experimenting with original ideas for pattern using pencil drawings, then finger paints.

3. Ask the children to make sketches of the trees.

4. Create a large tree collage. Make leaves by using tissue paper in different shades of green, dipped in PVA glue with black thread running through.

5. Discuss some familiar nursery rhymes with the children and choose one that can be linked to the book by changing some of the words.

6. Display the tree collage with the sketches and the new version of a traditional nursery rhyme.

A nursery rhyme composed by the Nursery, inspired by the book
"One, Two, Tree!"

Mary Mary quite contrary how does your green wood grow?

Mary Mary quite contrary how does your green wood grow?
With great big trunks, and lots of leaves
and tall trees all in row, row, row,
with tall trees all in a row.

Animals

Approach

1. Discuss the different animals that are represented in the story and choose four of them to study in more detail.

2. Cut out large animal shapes in brightly-coloured card and use finger painting with white paints to create a pattern.

3. Ask the children to write a cinquain poem about each animal and mount the poems on animal-shaped card. A cinquain poem has five lines and the first line could be the animal's name. The second line needs two words and could describe the animal's colours. The third line needs three words and could describe how the animal moves. The fourth line needs four words and could describe the animal's characteristics. The fifth line needs one word which has real impact and encapsulates the animal perfectly.

4. Display the cinquain poems with the animal paintings.

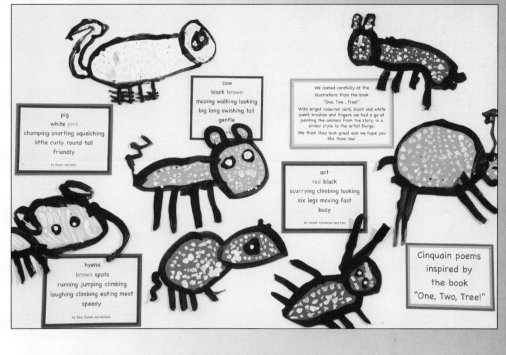

Resources
● Different coloured card
● White poster paint

Crowds

Approach

1. Visit a crowded place with the children, such as a shopping centre. Alternatively, arrange for a large group of children to walk in one direction, whilst a smaller group walks in the opposite direction. Discuss how it feels to be in a crowd. Photograph the scene.

2. Although all the animals in the story are drawn in a similar way, they have been depicted using different colours. Create a 3-D crowd scene using the photograph as a starting point. Children could make play dough people in different colours but with the same basic shape and embellish with glitter, buttons and sequins.

3. Cut one section from a cardboard box, and line the remaining areas with mirrors. Display the play dough crowd on a mirrored floor.

Resources
● Play dough in different colours
● Cardboard box and mirrors
● Digital camera
● Glitter, buttons and sequins

Australia – The Echidna and the Shade Tree

shiny Summer sun

rough red rocks

tall tree trunk

dry dusty desert

Read *The Echidna and the Shade Tree* told by Mona Green, illustrations adapted from paintings by Aboriginal children and compiled by Pamela Lofts (published by Scholastic). This is an Aboriginal story which tells of how the echidna got his spikes. There was once a huge tree in the middle of the desert, which gave shade to all the animals. While they all went out hunting, the old echidna stayed behind to look after the children. On the animals return with food, it was the children who got the tastiest bits and poor echidna only got the scraps. Because of their unkindness, echidna decides to get his revenge by pulling up the shade tree and moving it, which has dire consequences for him! The vivid illustrations in this story reflect the colours and the heat of the Australian desert.

A Desert Landscape

Approach

Resources
- Paint
- Sand
- PVA glue
- Glitter, sequins
- Gummed paper
- Red sugar paper

The Echidna got spikes in his back and he felt cross when they only gave him the scraps what the children didn't want to eat. He felt cross and sad and very, very unhappy when they chased him.

Rosalind

1. Discuss the desert landscape of Australia – the colours of the sand and the distant hills and the fierce heat of the sun. In this story the illustrations depict red mountains and a tree with very colourful foliage.

2. Make a display of the landscape with the blue sky and red 3-D mountains, use yellow paint mixed with sand and PVA glue for the sandy desert. The desert sun should be large and have glitter or sequins added for brightness. Place a large tree in the foreground with brightly coloured gummed paper torn into leaf shapes.

3. Brainstorm key words describing the landscape, for example, sparkling sun, red rocks and dusty desert.

4. Place on the display as labels.

Boomerangs

Approach

Resources
- Papier mache
- Paint

1. Discuss what a boomerang is – a curved, wooden shape, used by Aborigines, which can be thrown in such a way that it returns to its thrower. It is often seen as a symbol of Australia.

2. Groups of children could make a boomerang using papier mache. Paint and decorate with symbols.

3. Ask the children to choose a character or an object from the poem and to write a six-lined riddle about it.

A riddle is a poem which gives an interesting description of something without actually saying what it is. The poetry needs to have a magical quality and to be highly imaginative. Riddles work better if they are written in rhyming couplets. Words need to be chosen carefully so that it is not too easy to guess the subject matter.

The Echidna

Approach

1. Discuss what an echidna is and what it looks like – an Australia animal which eats ants and looks like a hedgehog with long spines.

2. Ask the children to each draw an echidna.

3. Collectively, make a large clay echidna.

Resources
- Clay
- Craft sticks
- PVA glue
- Paint
- Cartridge paper

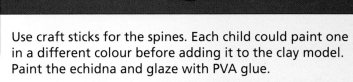

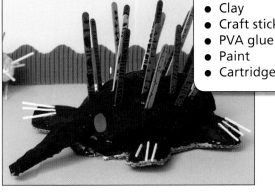

Use craft sticks for the spines. Each child could paint one in a different colour before adding it to the clay model. Paint the echidna and glaze with PVA glue.

4. Discuss what happened to the echidna in the story and why. Elicit the children's thoughts about the echidna's feelings.

5. Display the large echidna with the drawings.

Australia – Rainbow Bird

Read *Rainbow Bird* retold by Eric Maddern, illustrated by Adrienne Kennaway (published by Frances Lincoln). This Aboriginal folk tale is set in Dreamtime. Crocodile Man has something that no one else has – fire. He keeps the world dark and cold until one day Bird Woman takes her chance and snatches some of his firesticks while he sleeps. After placing fire into the hearts of all the trees, she puts firesticks into her tail and becomes the beautiful Rainbow Bird. Without his fire, Crocodile Man is consigned to living in the swamps whilst the Rainbow Bird flies high in the sky. The glowing illustrations depict the red earth and the warmth of the Australian landscape.

The Rainbow Bird

Approach

1. Discuss the appearance and features of Bird Woman at the beginning of the story - her dull colours and how she is cold and sad. Compare this with her

Rainbow Bird

Colourful
Rainbow bird
Dancing, blazing brightly.
Feathers sparkling like fire
Splendid.

Bird Woman

Black
Orange beaked
Perched up high
Watching, waiting, shivering cold.
Patient.

appearance as the Rainbow Bird – the warmth of her brightly-coloured feathers and confident posture.

2. Using watercolours, make a landscape of the sky with the sun as depicted in the story. Make 3-D collages of Bird Woman and the Rainbow Bird and place on the landscape background.

3. Write a class cinquain poem for each of the two birds to describe their colours and appearance. The poems should have five lines. For example, the first line of one word, the second line of two words, the third line of three words, the fourth line of four words and the final line of one word. Each line could focus on one aspect of the bird such as its colour, character and how it moves, with the final word an emotive or dramatic one.

Resources

- Watercolour paints
- Assorted coloured fabric
- Wadding
- Tissue and crepe paper

The Dreamtime

Approach

1. Discuss how the Australian Aborigines refer to the Creation as the Dreamtime and how they use stories to explain what happens in the world around them. Discuss the connection between the landscape and the Dreamtime stories which recount how scenery was created by animal or human action.

2. Ask the children to write a Dreamtime story about an animal or a bird associated with the Aboriginal culture and to describe how it got one of its features. For example, its colour, stripes or tail. Fold a piece of A3 sugar paper and mount the story inside and illustrate. Paint or draw a front cover for the story featuring the chosen creature and a title.

3. Look at examples of Aboriginal art featuring painted dots. Make colourful dot patterns on hand shapes and shapes of Australian reptiles, such as snakes, lizards and geckos using a stick dipped into paint.

4. Display the Dreamtime stories together with the dot patterns.

Resources
- A3 sugar paper in assorted colours
- Paint and crayons
- Sticks
- Black sugar paper

Bird Woman's Journey

Approach

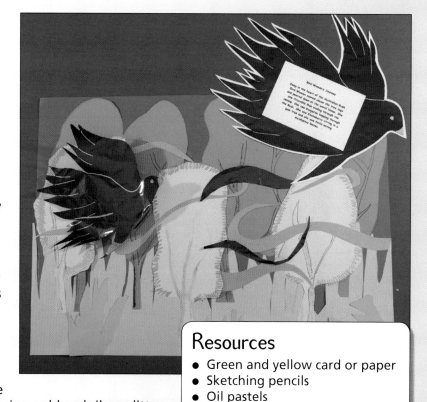

1. Look at the illustration of Bird Woman flying through the trees putting fire into the heart of them.

2. Ask each child to compose a short descriptive piece of writing to describe where Bird Woman flew when she put fire in the heart of the trees, and what she saw on her journey.

3. Create a similar scene of Bird Woman flying through the trees. Cut out large tree shapes using green and yellow card or paper. Add the detail of bark and branches on the green trees using sketching pencils. On the yellow trees use yellow oil pastels for the details and outline with gold pen. Place the green trees in the background interspersed with some yellow trees. Make Bird Woman using card and place on to the picture slightly raised. Create her fire trail using gold and silver glitter.

4. Display the descriptive writing with the picture.

Resources
- Green and yellow card or paper
- Sketching pencils
- Oil pastels
- Gold pen
- Gold and silver glitter

Australia – Wombat Goes Walkabout

Read *Wombat Goes Walkabout* by Michael Morpurgo, illustrated by Christian Birmingham (published by Collins). One day Wombat, who loves digging, digs a big hole and then climbs inside to sit and think in the dark. Later, when he climbs out, his mother has gone and he is all alone in the Australian bush. While searching for his mother, he meets Kookaburra, Wallaby, Possum, Emu, Boy and Koala. The creatures are all rather dismissive of Wombat's digging skills but when the danger of fire threatens, it is Wombat's special skill that saves them. When Wombat is finally reunited with his mother and she asks him what he has been doing, he is so relieved to find her that he tells her that he has just been digging and thinking! The beautiful illustrations reflect the colours and the heat of the Australian landscape.

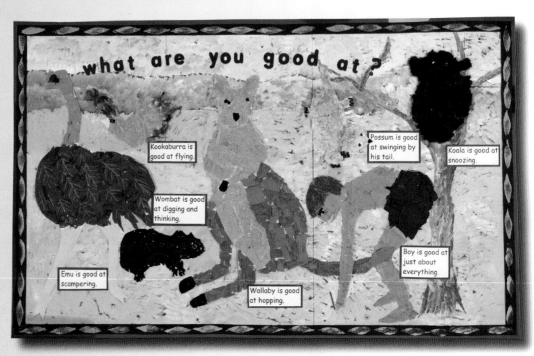

The Wombat

Approach

Resources
- A variety of collage materials
- Paint and glue
- Sugar paper

1. Discuss what a wombat is – its appearance, where it lives and its habits. Discuss the Australian bush and the other animals in the story – the kookaburra, wallaby, possum, emu and koala.

2. Discuss how all the creatures in the story have a particular strength. For example, the kookaburra can fly and the possum can hang upside down and swing by his tail.

3. Discuss the children's strengths and talents. Make a class book of paintings showing what the children are good at. Add speech bubbles explaining the children's talents.

4. Make a large display of all the characters featured in the story – wombat digging, kookaburra flying, wallaby hopping, possum hanging upside down by his tail, emu scampering, boy drawing in the sand and koala dozing in her eucalyptus tree. Use a variety of collage materials. Add the title 'What are you good at?' Make large labels for each of the characters saying what they are good at.

5. Place the class book in front of the display.

Lost and Found

Approach

Resources
- Cardboard boxes
- Scissors and glue
- Paint
- Clay

1. Discuss how Wombat goes off to dig his deep hole and then when he climbs out, he realises that he has lost his mother. Discuss how he feels and his mother's reaction at the end of the story when she finds him (she hugs him). Look at the final illustration – nothing else is important because Wombat has found his mother.

2. Ask the children to write a short story using the title 'Lost and found'. The story could be about an object that was lost and then found again. The story could be from the children's own experience or an imaginary one.

3. Each child could design and make a container to keep something precious safe so that it does not get lost. Paint and embellish.

4. Display the stories together with the containers.

Aboriginal Art

Approach

1. Explain that the boy in the story is an Aborigine. Look at and discuss the illustration in the story where he is drawing a picture of an emu in the sand.

2. Ask the children to use books and the Internet to look at examples of Aboriginal art and use their findings as inspiration for creating a large picture in this style.

3. Make a large picture on cotton which reflects Aboriginal culture. Use a thick black felt pen for outlining Aboriginal images and patterns. Add colour by infilling with fingerprint painting and dots. Make a border of snakes, again using a dark outline filled with dots and fingerprints.

4. Display the picture as a wall hanging.

Resources
- Large piece of cotton fabric
- Thick black felt pen
- Paint

USA – Brother Eagle, Sister Sky

Read *Brother Eagle, Sister Sky*, paintings by Susan Jeffers (published by Puffin).Chief Seattle lived from approximately 1790 to 1866. The text in this book is taken from a powerful speech delivered by Chief Seattle to the government in Washington. It conveys the message that our environment is precious and that it must be cherished and treated with the utmost respect. However, if we neglect the earth, we do so at our own peril. Images depicted in this beautifully illustrated book reinforce this powerful message of conservation and environmental awareness. The paintings also reflect both the beauty of nature and the devastating effects that neglect and mistreatment can have on the landscape.

Chief Seattle's People

Approach

1. Discuss how Chief Seattle stresses the importance of family and ancestors to the Native Americans and how his people cherished their land.

2. Use a variety of materials to produce a collage with Native American images such as canoes, tepees, headdresses, feathers and arrows.

3. Write a class poem about the importance of the land to Chief Seattle's people.

4. Display the collage with the poem.

Resources
- A variety of textiles
- Coloured paper
- Beads and buttons

Contrasting Landscapes

Approach

1. Discuss Chief Seattle's fears for the future and especially his concerns about environmental awareness, conservation, freedom of choice and justice.

2. Ask each child to write an article for a newspaper in response to Chief Seattle's speech, from the point of view of a child who is not a Native American (perhaps the child seen with Chief Seattle on the front cover of the book). The article would need to address Chief Seattle's concerns for the future. Display with illustrations.

3. The children could write a persuasive letter to the council highlighting a local environmental issue.

4. On a piece of A3 paper, paint a landscape scene with mountains and trees in the background and a river in the foreground. On this painting place a canoe on the river, 3-D tepees, a colourful totem pole and Native Americans in traditional costume.

Resources
- Oil pastels
- Charcoal
- White chalk pastels
- A3 cartridge paper

5. On another piece of A3 paper, paint the same setting with mountains in the background and a river in the foreground. This time show the effects of neglect and pollution on the landscape. Using charcoal and white pastels paint blackened tree stumps. Place bottles, rubbish and discarded objects in the river.

6. Display the two paintings side by side (see page 58).

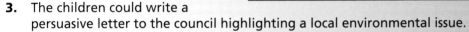

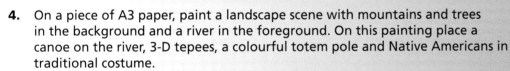

Chief Seattle's Land

Approach

1. Discuss how Chief Seattle and his people lived in harmony with nature and focus on the different parts of the earth that are mentioned, such as the trees, the flowers, the birds, the animals, the streams and the rivers.

2. Ask the children to choose one aspect of nature as depicted in the book and write an acrostic poem about it. An acrostic poem is one in which the first or the last letters of each line spell a word that links in with the subject matter of the poem. Set the scene by playing some tranquil music with sounds from nature perhaps birds' song or the cascading sound of water.

3. Each child could make a background watercolour painting for the poems which links the images from nature as described in the poetry.

Resources
- Watercolour paints
- Music

USA – Lord of the Animals

Read *Lord of the Animals* retold and illustrated by Fiona French (published by Frances Lincoln). This Native American creation myth tells how Coyote, having created the world and its animals, gathers a council to decide how to make the Lord of all the animals. The animals cannot agree and after listening to their ideas, Coyote suggests they each make a clay model of the Lord and he will choose the best one. However, what the animals do not realise is that crafty Coyote has his own plan! Most of this story is presented as a dialogue between Coyote and the animals. The pattern in the story is enhanced by the highly patterned illustrations of the animals and the landscape.

Pattern and Design

Approach

1. Discuss how the highly patterned illustrations and the story reflect the Native American culture in a very vivid way. Look at the use of colour in the patterns and how it emphasises the different parts of the landscape. For example, greens and blues are used to depict the running water. In contrast the patterned fish stand out because they are black and white.

2. Make a poly block print using one of the animal images in the story. Use a sharp pencil to draw the design onto the block. Print and then draw more detail on the block. Using a different colour ink, print on top of the original.

3. Ask the children to write a brief review of the story, including comments on the illustrations, to be presented at a book club meeting. Encourage use of emotive language, complex sentences and pose rhetorical questions. Grab the reader's attention with an eye-catching title.

4. Display the poly block prints with the reviews.

Resources
- Poly blocks
- Printing ink and rollers
- Sharp pencils
- Coloured paper, tissue paper and card
- Fabric

Animals

Approach

1. Discuss the variety of animals depicted in the story, with a focus on their physical appearance.

Resources
- Calico squares
- Threads
- Fabric paint

2. Make an animal textile painting using one of the animals from the story. Embellish with stitching.

3. Ask the children to research one of the animals from the story using the Internet or non-fiction books. They should look for information about the habitat, home, food and behaviour of the chosen animal, and present this in the form of a fact file cube.

4. Display the fact files with the animal textile paintings.

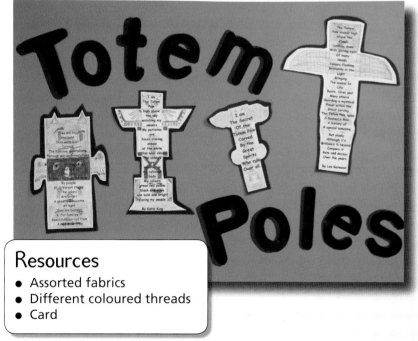

Symbols

Approach

1. Discuss the Native American artefacts depicted in the story (beads, headbands, feathers, tepees and fringed garments). Find out about other Native American symbols. Discuss the significance of the Totem Pole in Native American culture (a carved wooden pole representing their family kinships and stories). Look at pictures of Totem Poles and discuss the pattern, colour and shapes.

2. Design and make a section of a fabric Totem Pole using a variety of colours and fabrics. Place the sections together to make a complete Totem Pole.

3. Ask the children to write a thin poem using a few words per line which describes the significance of the Totem Pole in Native American culture. Children could write the poems either from the point of view of a Native American Indian or from their own point of view. Include a visual description of the shape, colours and patterns of the Totem Pole.

4. Display the poems, mounted on Totem Pole shapes, with the fabric Totem Poles.

Resources
- Assorted fabrics
- Different coloured threads
- Card

61

Tobago – Gregory Cool

Read *Gregory Cool* by Caroline Binch (published by Frances Lincoln). This charming story is set on the Caribbean island of Tobago. The vibrant and realistic illustrations convey a real sense of place. The vegetation, the beach and the palm trees with coconuts give an exotic feel to the story and reflect a far more simple way of life. The key character, Gregory, visits his grandparents in Tobago but, at first, he finds the culture so completely different that he feels unsure in his new surroundings. In his grandparents' house there are no televisions or computer games, the food is very spicy and his cousin, Lennox, does not even wear shoes! During a picnic on the beach with his grandparents and Lennox, Gregory meets some friendly fishermen who give him a gift of a large, red fish and invite him to go fishing with them. Finally, Gregory starts to feel at home and, towards the end of the story, as he watches the moon rise, surrounded by the beauty of nature, he kicks his trainers off.

The Island

Approach

1. Discuss the similarities and differences between life in Tobago and life in the UK. Focus on the differences between the houses and the landscapes. In this story, Gregory's grandparents' house is a simple, traditional one with a tin, corrugated roof. Steps lead up to the front door because the house is raised from the ground to enable the air to circulate underneath the building to keep it cool.

2. Discuss the climate in Tobago and the wonderful beaches there.

3. Ask the children to design a poster which advertises Tobago as an ideal holiday destination. Use persuasive language and alliteration to encourage holiday makers to visit. The posters should be colourful and depict a typical scene in Tobago that will entice readers to want to visit such a beautiful island.

Resources
- Pastels
- A3 cartridge paper
- Tissue paper
- Foil paper

Gregory

Approach

1. Discuss Gregory's visit to his grandparents and how, as time goes by, his attitude towards their way of life changes.

2. The children could write a journal from Gregory's point of view which describes both the events during his holiday and his feelings.

3. Make a large display showing a beach scene from the story using a variety of materials, reflecting the Caribbean environment. Make large palm trees with 3-D sugar paper branches.

4. Display the journals with the collage.

Resources
- Collage materials
- Sugar paper

The Fishermen

Approach

1. Ask the children to use the Internet to find out about the sort of jobs people have on a small Caribbean island like Tobago.

2. Discuss how the fishermen in the story help Gregory to feel more settled.

3. The children could write a Caribbean style menu using the food mentioned in the story as a guide and illustrate.

4. Make 3-D fish from plastic bottles, painted red. Use gold and silver metallic pens to highlight the scales on the fish. Design and make large leaves from a selection of green paper.

5. Display the colourful menus with the fish wrapped up in the paper leaves.

Resources
- Acrylic paints
- Plastic bottles
- A selection of green paper
- Silver and gold metallic pens

The Amazon – The Shaman's Apprentice

Read *The Shaman's Apprentice* by Lynne Cherry and Mark J Plotkin, illustrated by Lynne Cherry (published by Voyager books). This story is set in the riverside village of Kwamala, deep in the Amazon rainforest. When Kamanya is ill with a fever, his mother takes him to the Shaman (medicine man). The Shaman collects leaves, roots and bark from the forest which he boils up to make medicine for Kamanya. The next day the fever has disappeared and over the years as Kamanya grows up, he never forgets that the Shaman saved his life and begins to learn his skill. Then one day the villagers fall ill and the Shaman is unable to make them better. When missionaries arrive in the village they bring pills for the malaria-stricken people and the Shaman loses his place of honour in the tribe. Gradually life changes and the years pass, then one day a young woman arrives by canoe and the Shaman's self-esteem and place of honour is restored. The beautifully detailed illustrations of the plant life convey a real sense of the rainforest.

Landscape

Approach

1. Locate the Amazon Rainforest in an atlas or on a globe. Discuss the huge size of this geographical area. Discuss the lifestyle of the Tirio tribe in the village of Kwamala as depicted at the beginning of the story.

2. Discuss the routine lives of the people in the village. For example, Kamanya's mother and sisters wash clothes in the river, grow cotton which is spun into cloth, grind berries to dye the cloth and make bread; his father hunts for tapir and Kamanya swims in the river and plays in the forest. Ask the children to write, in the first person, about a day in the life of one of the villagers.

3. Make a 3-D model of the village of Kwamala at the side of a river. Make the huts, rainforest trees, river with some rocks in, and canoes out of a variety of materials.

4. Display the writing with the model village.

Resources

- Atlas or globe
- Piece of board
- Small sticks or straws
- Tissue paper
- Shiny foil
- Sand
- Card
- Plasticine or modelling clay

Plant life

Approach

1. Discuss how at the beginning of the story, Kamanya's fever is healed by the Shaman's medicine made of leaves, roots and bark from the rainforest.

2. Using the Internet, children could research medicines that are made from plants and find out about the healing properties of plants.

3. Present the information in the shape of a medicine bottle or a plant.

4. Look at the detailed illustrations of plant life in the book. Ask the children to sketch flowers and leaves, using pencils and oil pastels. Using photographs of the different plants found in the rainforest as a starting point, make individual fabric collages of the brightly coloured flowers. Use vivelle and felt on a hessian square and embellish with buttons, sequins, pipe cleaners and glitter.

5. Display the fabric collages as wall hangings, with the sketches, oil pastel drawings and written information.

Resources
- Cartridge paper
- Sketching pencils
- Oil pastels
- Hessian
- Sewing threads and needles
- Vivelle and felt
- Sequins, buttons and glitter
- Coloured pipe cleaners

The Rainforest

Approach

1. Discuss the features and characteristics of a rainforest – the lush growth, exotic flowers, rich plant life and brightly coloured birds.

2. Discuss the people who live there and what they wear. For example, due to the climate the people do not wear many clothes. However, the chief or head of the tribes' headdress is often large and very colourful.

3. Look at the illustration where the chief is talking to Gabriela and discuss his headdress – what it is made of and how it is made. Design and make a headdress for a chief that reflects the colours and wildlife of the rainforest. Use brightly coloured feathers, coloured card and pipe cleaners.

4. Ask the children to write a piece describing what influenced the design of their headdress and how it was made.

5. Display the headdresses with the writing.

Resources
- Brightly coloured feathers in assorted sizes
- Coloured card
- Pipe cleaners
- Scissors and glue

The Galapagos Islands – We're Sailing to Galapagos

The Giant Tortoise

The giant tortoise with his green patterned shell
Moves along plodding, plodding, plodding.
The giant tortoise is a hundred years old
Munches his food as he crawls along slowly, slowly, slowly.

Read *We're Sailing to Galapagos: A Week in the Pacific*, by Laurie Krebs, illustrated by Grazia Restelli (published by Barefoot Books). This story is a day-by-day account of all the different creatures seen by two children who are going on a special journey in a sailboat to the Galapagos Islands. The text is very simple and uses rhyme and repetition to tell the story as well as a repeated chorus at the end of every two pages. At the end of the story, there is some interesting factual information about the Galapagos Islands, the creatures of the Galapagos and a section about Charles Darwin's visit to the islands. The eye-catching illustrations are made from cut out card in a variety of colours and textures placed together in a similar way to a collage.

The Giant Tortoises

Approach

1. Discuss how the giant tortoises are the symbol of the Galapagos Islands. Inform the class that, as some of the tortoises are over a hundred years old, they are the largest tortoises in the world.

2. Make a giant tortoise using a selection of green and brown fabric of different shades and textures. Draw an outline of a tortoise on a large piece of card and place fabric pieces on to the card to represent the pattern on the tortoise's shell. Add feet and head using coloured card and tissue paper.

3. Ask the children to write a four line poem which describes the appearance of a giant tortoise. Focus on powerful verbs which convey how a giant tortoise moves. Include some repetition.

4. Display the large tortoise with the poems.

Resources

- A2 thick white card
- A selection of green and brown fabric
- Coloured card
- Tissue paper

Journey to Galapagos

Approach

1. Ask each child to make a zigzag book with a page for each day of the week and draw the animal or bird that the two children in the story meet on that day.

2. Ask the children to write a sentence about each animal or bird featured in the story and place these in the zigzag book. If possible, they should type their work on the computer.

3. Mount a display board by dividing it into three sections. Cut painted blue paper in a curve for the sky, dark blue for the sea and chocolate brown for the shore. Make a variety of animals featured in the story using assorted collage materials. Place the animals on the appropriate section on the display board.

4. Make labels for the different animals and place on the display.

5. Display the zigzag books in front of the large collage.

Resources
- A3 paper
- Collage materials
- Card for zigzag books
- Paint

The Landscape

Approach

1. Explain how the Galapagos Islands have been formed from underwater volcanoes at different times and how they have different wildlife and plant life.

2. Create a 3-D scene of one of the Galapagos Islands. Using a large piece of plywood as the base draw the outline of an island. Paint the outer section blue for the sea. Create the natural features of the island by using scrunched up newspaper covered with masking tape to form the basic shape of rocks and a volcano. Build up the features with mod rock and paint the volcano and rocks black and grey. Make some animals or birds that live on the island in clay, using buttons in different shapes and sizes for decorating them.

3. Ask the children to make a simple poster informing the reader of the special attractions in the Galapagos Islands. Place a bold heading on the poster and use vibrant colours and illustrations to reflect the islands' natural features. Use emotive language with short pithy sentences and make the poster eye-catching with a clever logo.

4. Display the island scene with the poster.

Resources
- Mod rock, newspaper and masking tape
- A large piece of plywood
- Paint
- Clay
- Buttons in a variety of shapes

Chile – Mariana and the Merchild

Read *Mariana and the Merchild* by Caroline Pitcher, illustrated by Jackie Morris (published by Frances Lincoln). In this delightful folk tale from Chile, the main character, Mariana, is an old woman who lives alone in a hut by the sea. She longs for friendship but the village children pull faces at her and run away. One morning after a ferocious storm, she finds a crab in a rock pool and takes it home for supper. However, instead of a crab inside the shell, she finds a merbaby. Although Mariana loves the merbaby, she realises that she must return her to the sea. Through her unselfishness and kindness Mariana not only gains the trust of the merchild but also the devoted friendship of the village children. The use of figurative language and simile makes the setting both vibrant and vivid. The evocative illustrations, which reflect the detailed patterns and colours of Chile, enhance this enchanting tale.

Natural Objects

Approach

1. Discuss the variety of natural objects found on the sea shore after a storm, such as driftwood, pebbles and shells.

2. Ask the children to make sketches of pebbles using shading to create depth and texture. Cut out the individual pebbles, overlap and arrange to create a composition.

3. Play the extract *Fortuna* from *Carmina Baruna* by Carl Orff which describes the different stages of a storm. Listen to the dynamics of the piece, which starts off quietly and gets louder as the storm progresses.

4. Brainstorm the use of musical instruments to reflect the stages of the storm and link to the story (Indian bells, chime bars and triangles could be played softly and drums, gongs, wood blocks and cymbals could be played louder and faster to reflect the mood of the storm). Practise using these instruments.

5. Play the music again and, at the same time, children could write a descriptive piece starting with the onset of the storm at the beginning of the story and leading to the tranquillity after it has abated.

6. Present a performance to an audience combining reading the children's descriptive writing and playing the musical instruments to reflect mood and pace.

7. Display the writing with a selection of natural objects.

Resources
- A selection of smooth pebbles and other natural objects
- Sketch pencils
- Cartridge paper
- Musical instruments

Contrasting Moods

Approach

Resources
- A3 cartridge paper and colouring pencils
- Craft tools for making rag cushions
- Hessian squares and recycled fabric

1. Brainstorm a range of emotions covered in the story and link with corresponding colours, such as red for anger, yellow for happiness, blue for sorrow and green for serenity.

2. Look at some of Kandinsky's paintings and in particular at his use of symbols and how he linked colour and shape closely with emotions.

3. Ask the children to sketch patterns or designs using symbols, colour and shape to reflect different feelings, for example friendship, loneliness, happiness, humility, fear and courage.

4. Make a mood board by dividing A3 cartridge paper into eight sections and transfer the sketch designs on to the different sections of the cartridge paper and then add colour.

5. Using the mood boards as a starting point, choose a section linked to friendship as a basic design for making rag cushions.

6. Copy a design on to a square of hessian and using strips of recycled fabric (for example rubber gloves, old t-shirts, netting etc.) make a rag rug. Use the rag rug to make a cushion.

7. Ask the children to choose a favourite colour and use it as a title for a short poem. Take an abstract approach with a focus on the general effect of the colour and the emotions associated with it. Use figurative language such as simile, personification, alliteration and onomatopoeia to create a vivid image.

8. Display the mood boards with the rag rugs.

Red

Red is anger and rage,
Frustration and unhappiness
It surrounds me when I am angry, annoyed.
It is the fire that burns and destroys.

Friendship

Approach

Resources
- Embroidery threads

1. Discuss how Mariana's life is transformed after she finds the merchild – from one of loneliness to one that is rich in friendship.

2. Ask the children to write a personal letter from Mariana to the merchild expressing the happiness that their friendship has brought her. Write in the first person using a conversational tone. Pose questions and be very enthusiastic and friendly (use exclamation marks and question marks). Illustrate using images from the story.

3. Children could make a friendship bracelet using embroidery threads plaited together.

4. Display the letters with the friendship bracelets.

Peru – From Beans To Batteries

Read *From Beans To Batteries* by Steve Bruce, illustrated by Annie Kubler (published by Child's Play International Ltd). This story is about Aldomaro, a young boy who lives in a village high in the Andes, in Peru. His ambition is to be a doctor and so he never misses 'Doctor Manami's Half Hour' on the radio. But one day his radio stops working – the batteries have run out! In order to buy some new batteries, Aldomaro and his sister have to pick beans to take to sell at the market, which is a two hour walk away. Finally, after their long walk, they reach the market in Bambamarco. Just as they are giving up hope of selling their beans, a kind stallholder comes to their rescue. The illustrations feature the typical landscape of the Andes – the mountainous terrain with the villages in the valleys and show the women in their traditional dress with their shawls and hats.

Landscape

Approach

Resources
- Atlas or globe
- A variety of collage materials
- Paint and glue
- Clay

1. Find South America and Peru on a map or a globe. Discuss the features – the mountains, types of houses, food, transport, people, animals and plant life.

2. Ask each child to choose one aspect and present it on an information sheet with illustrations.

3. Using a variety of materials, make a large collage showing Aldomaro and his sister on their journey home from market, listening to their radio. Include mountains in the background, some vegetation, llamas, houses on the hillside and a man and woman walking ahead with their donkey. Make small clay houses to place in front of the collage as part of the display.

4. Display some of the information facts on the collage.

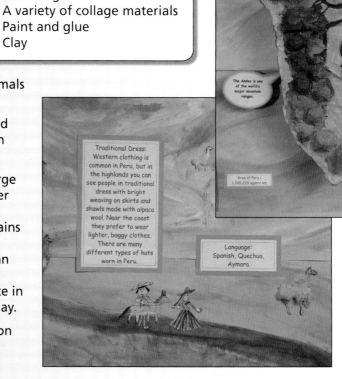

Food and Agriculture

Approach

1. Look at the illustrations in the story and discuss the different fruit and vegetables, animals and the people working with them. For example, at the beginning of the story two little girls are taking the husks off corn on the cob and Aldomaro's father is sorting potatoes. On the way to market Aldomaro and his sister pass sheep and cattle, and at the market in Bambamarca, a lady is selling red hot chillies and many other vegetables.

Peruvian Food:
The main types of food eaten in Peru are potatoes, corn, hot peppers, rice, beans, onions, fish and tropical fruits.

Agricultural products:
Coffee, cotton, sugarcane, rice, wheat, plantains, coca poultry, beef, dairy products wool & fish

Currency: Nuevo Sol

2. Using the Internet and the library, the children could research the food and agriculture of Peru.

3. Make a model scene with people and tables with pots and containers of food. For authenticity place pieces of real corn in some of the dishes! Dress the figures in typical Peruvian clothes as depicted in the story.

4. Display the model scene with Peruvian food facts and agriculture information.

Resources
- Pipe cleaners
- Collage materials
- Clay
- Card and paints

Resources
- Cardboard boxes and junk modelling materials
- Paint and glue
- Shiny foil
- Assorted batteries

Batteries:
We have made models of items you can find today that are powered by batteries:
CD player, torch, TV, MP3, remote control, game boy, child's computer, clock, watch, camera, toy car, mobile phone and a radio.

Batteries

Approach

1. Discuss how Aldomaro needed batteries for his radio to work.

2. Make a class list of all the different things that require batteries in order to work.

3. Using cardboard boxes and other junk modelling materials make 3-D models of things that use batteries. For example, CD and cassette recorders, torches, radios, alarm clocks, radio controlled toys, cameras and mobile phones. Paint and add details to the models.

4. Display the models with the lists and an assortment of real batteries of different shapes and sizes.

What is our troll like?
What does he look like?
What does he like to do?
What does he eat?
Where does he live?

Norway – The Three Billy Goats Gruff (page 8)